T H E **PARADOX** O F ASSET PRICING

FRONTIERS OF ECONOMIC RESEARCH

Series Editors

David M. Kreps

Thomas J. Sargent

Paul Klemperer

THE **PARADOX** OF
ASSET PRICING

PETER BOSSAERTS

PRINCETON UNIVERSITY PRESS   PRINCETON AND OXFORD

Library of Congress Cataloging-in-Publication Data

Bossaerts, Peter L., 1960–

    The paradox of asset pricing / Peter Bossaerts.

      p.   cm.—(Frontiers of economic research)

    Includes bibliographical references and index.

    ISBN 0-691-09029-7 (CL : alk. paper)

    1. Capital assets pricing model. 2. Efficient market theory. 3. Securities. I. Title.

II. Series.

HG4636 .B67   2002

332.6—dc21   2001055194

British Library Cataloging-in-Publication Data is available

This book has been composed in New Baskerville

Printed on acid-free paper.∞

www.pup.princeton.edu

Printed in the United States of America

10 9 8 7 6 5 4 3 2 1

CONTENTS

I   Principles of Asset-Pricing Theory

Wherein we review the basics of asset-pricing theory, starting from dynamic programming (pointing out some of the surprising simplifications when applied to portfolio analysis), introducing the notion of equilibrium, and then narrowing everything down to arrive at the Capital Asset-Pricing Model (CAPM). The emphasis is on the features that the CAPM shares with virtually all other asset-pricing models, namely, in equilibrium, prices are set so that expected excess returns are proportional to covariance with aggregate risk.

2   Empirical Methodology

Empirical tests of asset-pricing theory require the researcher to make auxiliary assumptions that are not necessarily an integral part of the theory. Most prominent is the assumption that ties ex-ante beliefs (which determine prices) to the ex-post frequencies of the payoffs, which has become known as the efficient markets hypothesis (EMH). EMH dramatically simplifies empirical methodology. We review three important types of tests that it generated: (1) Tests of the mean-variance efficiency of benchmark portfolio(s); (2) stochastic Euler equation tests; and (3) variance bounds tests.

3   The Empirical Evidence in a Nutshell

An anthology of the extensive literature on tests of asset-pricing models enables us to form a fairly comprehensive image of the empirical evidence. Few would be encouraged by the results.

4   The Experimental Evidence

But perhaps we are demanding too much from empirical studies of historical data from field markets. What about the evidence from simple, purposely built experimental markets? Some principles emerge well and alive (e.g., the CAPM), others can be rejected outright (e.g., instantaneous equilibration). The lab also allows us to discover things that are fundamental to economic theory but difficult to detect in historical data, such as the ranking of Arrow-Debreu securities prices. At the same time, we experience how hard it is to control beliefs.

5   From EMH to Merely Efficient Learning

Although we obviously do not yet understand how to extrapolate lab results to the giant and complex field markets, we can investigate whether our econometric methodology has not been the cause of the empirical failure of asset-pricing theory. The first suspect is EMH. The criticism will be constructive, by demonstrating that EMH is unnecessarily strong: much of the simplicity of the EMH-based empirical methodology can be retained even if one cuts out the most objectionable part. We develop a new methodology for testing asset-pricing models that allows the market to hold mistaken expectations at times, but still requires it to learn as under EMH. We will call it the hypothesis of efficiently learning markets (ELM).

6   Revisiting the Historical Record

Armed with new tools, we can revisit historical data. We investigate the aftermarket performance of almost five thousand U.S. initial public offerings (IPOs) in the period 1975–95. Although not perfect, we find far more support for the theory. The example suggests that we may want to substitute ELM for EMH in future studies of historical data from field markets.

PREFACE

It is a very beautiful line of reasoning.

The only problem is that perhaps it is not true.

(After all, nature does not *have* to go along with our reasoning.)

—Richard P. Feynman, in *Lectures on Physics*

The purpose of this book is to explore the scientific achievements of finance over the past forty years. That is, we will investigate whether finance has improved our understanding of financial markets. The book is based on a series of lectures, first given in Oslo, Norway, in June, 1999.

It seems that modern finance is most successful when it is asked to create tools to improve financial decisionmaking in an inherently uncertain world. The term *financial engineering* is appropriate here. Dynamic hedging (and its pricing counterpart, options or fixed-income pricing) is a prime example. Its successes derive of course from the ability of the underlying econometric description to model adequately the regularities in price behavior (e.g., stochastic volatility). But the real meaning or even the economic sense of the econometric descriptions has not yet been explained. The statistical approach reflects an agnostic attitude similar to the one often encountered in the medical sciences, and driven by, perhaps, the urgency of the situation (an investment decision has to be made now).

In this book, we will rather be interested in: *why?* The goal is a deeper understanding of the workings of financial markets, not just a statistical description of their history.

Modern finance has generated a set of formal models of the workings of financial markets that certainly excel in terms of mathematical elegance. But abstract beauty and logical appeal do not guarantee scientific validity. The illustrious late Richard Feynman, professor of physics at Caltech, made the same observation when he discussed the derivation of the law of gravitational potential energy from the axiom of conservation of energy (see the above quote). Fortunately for physicists, there is ample evidence that the law of gravitational potential energy is correct (to a certain degree). In contrast, there appears to be surprisingly little scientific support for even the most widely used financial model, namely, the Capital Asset-Pricing Model (CAPM). One can sympathize with Fama and French (1996): they have recently begun to promote a pricing model that is based entirely on statistical regularities, begging the question of why it is more successful.

To put this differently, asset pricing is paradoxical. On the one hand, the theory is so persuasive that it is widely believed to be correct, to the point that business and both the executive and jurisdictional parts of government appeal to it. Yet there is little evidence that the theory explains the past, let alone that it predicts the future. This book is meant to explore what we really know to be empirically valid, that is, to what extent we can go beyond believing in the mathematics.

We will not be content with casual empirical support. For instance, the ubiquitous finding that stock prices are largely unpredictable is not sufficient ground to certify the rationality of stock markets. Would we want to maintain that a drunken person is rational simply because his path is unpredictable? Lack of predictability may merely reflect how ignorant we are. We will leave no taboos unexamined in this book. Even something as sacrosanct as instantaneous equilibration will be subject to rigorous validation (and found wanting). But in the end, we will be able to recognize a few basic principles that appear to be correct.

We will study the pricing of risk that is allocated through competitive markets, because that is what the empirical tests of asset pricing have focused on so far. Asset-pricing theory also makes predictions about the nature of the eventual allocation, but these have not been of much concern in empirical tests, so neither will they be of importance in this book. Similarly, there is an interesting theory of asset pricing under dispersed information, which addresses such issues as information aggregation, but the resulting pricing models have yet to be tested, perhaps because there is an issue as to whether they restrict aggregate data (e.g., prices and volume) at all. And so, we will also ignore asset pricing under asymmetric information.

The review of theory and evidence in this book is obviously selective. This does not mean that we must be insensitive to the literature that is omitted. The chosen material, however, makes a point that is often overlooked by critics of modern finance, which is the following.

Financial economists prefer to test their theories on historical data-sets. This is a very challenging way of assessing scientific value. Historical financial-market data come with subtle selection biases, they reflect the expectations of the period they cover, and they have to be understood against an incredibly complex background about which the empiricist has little information. On reflection, it would seem that tests of asset-pricing theories on historical data are doomed. Quite to the contrary, however, financial economists have managed to develop a statistical methodology that is remarkably robust and requires surprisingly little information about the historical environment.

It should be understood that this was accomplished at the cost of a strong auxiliary assumption, namely, the efficient markets hypothesis (EMH). The book will interpret EMH to mean that investors' ex ante beliefs are unbiased, and that the data are stationary. (This is not the standard definition, but the standard definition is vague; this book's definition reflects what has *actually* been tested.) EMH has become the target of criticism of the behavioral finance literature, starting with DeBondt and Thaler (1985).

This book addresses the question whether EMH can be relaxed without losing the old methodology's robustness and sparse use of data. EMH can indeed be relaxed in this way. The book will illustrate that the new methodology can easily overcome past objections to asset-pricing models. This suggests that the poor empirical record of asset-pricing theory is attributable to EMH (thereby confirming the behavioral finance critics), and not to the models themselves.

Financial economists' insistence on testing their theories only on historical data is rare among scientists. Imagine if physicists were to insist on testing only on histories of naturally falling objects that the acceleration caused by gravity is a constant 9.8 m/s^2! The task would be complex, even if one applies the right statistics to filter the many potential biases that are obviously going to be present (e.g., friction). Instead, a physicist's inclination is to first test in the laboratory.

This book invites the reader to think about the viability and meaning of experimentation as an alternative way to verify the principles of asset-pricing theory. It is obviously wrong to assert that finance is in no need of experiments because there are plenty of field data. Such an assertion reflects a confusion between data and information. Like many sciences, we have a great deal of field data. But we just do not yet know what to make of them.

Once it is accepted that experiments can be useful, the question is how to organize them to make them informative. The primary goal is to determine unambiguously whether asset-pricing theory is capable of making valid predictions at all. This requires simplicity, a feature rarely found in field markets. Hence, the intention is certainly not to build experimental markets that mimic field markets. Simplicity, however, should not be confounded with lack of realism. The experimental markets are no less real than field markets. They are real markets, where real people make real trades to earn (or lose) real money.

In fact, certain questions about asset-pricing theory can only be answered unambiguously in experimental markets. The core concept of modern finance is that markets equilibrate. In the field, one can only reject (as opposed to confirm) that markets have equilibrated, and then in only one way: by demonstrating that there were arbitrage opportunities (riskfree, zero-investment portfolios that generate strictly positive profits at times, but never generate losses). These opportunities rarely, if ever, happen and hence, the test is not very powerful.

Perhaps one day financial economists will be able to identify parameters that make a particular (equilibrium) asset-pricing model fit some historical market data. One may argue that this constitutes conclusive proof that the market equilibrated. It does not, because the validity of the parameters themselves cannot be cross-checked. For example, one may discover that a particular benchmark portfolio makes the CAPM explain postwar U.S. stock-market data. Because it will never be clear whether the chosen benchmark portfolio really is the market portfolio, such a finding would be no proof of equilibration (let alone of the CAPM).[1]

In contrast, the market portfolio is part of the design in a financial markets experiment, and therefore, is unambiguously known, which means that a genuine test of the CAPM becomes possible. In this book, we will discuss results from experiments that were meant to study the predictive power of the CAPM.

Many people helped shape the contents of the lectures on which this book is based. Foremost, there is the audience at the Norwegian School of Management where the lectures were first given. The students at Caltech subsequently worked their way through rough drafts of the lectures. Among them, I specially thank Elena Asparouhova. Colleagues also provided critical input, in particular, Pierre Hillion, Ravi Jagannathan, Richard Roll, and William Ziemba. My views on experiments have obviously been heavily shaped through countless discussions with my colleagues inside and outside the Division of Humanities and Social Sciences at Caltech, in particular, with Charles Plott. Of course, none of these people necessarily agrees with everything or even anything I have written here.

---

1. The informed reader will recognize this as the Roll critique. We will discuss the Roll critique in more detail in Chapter 1.

THE **PARADOX** OF ASSET PRICING

Principles of Asset-Pricing Theory

1.1 Introduction

In this chapter, we will study the body of asset-pricing theory that is most appropriate to understanding the empirical tests that are reported later in this book. In particular, we focus on the discrete-time, stationary dynamic asset-pricing models that have been derived over the past thirty years or so. There are other classes of asset-pricing models, such as Merton's continuous-time model (see Merton [1973]), but these have been less important in empirical analysis. The models we will consider here capture the essence of all modern asset-pricing theory, namely, that financial markets equilibrate to the point that expected returns are determined solely by covariance with aggregate risk.

Such static models as the Capital Asset-Pricing Model (CAPM) can be considered special cases. We focus on the dynamic models because they potentially explain the (albeit small) predictability that one can find in historical securities return data. Moreover, returns are usually measured as tomorrow's price plus dividend divided by today's price. It is customary in static asset-pricing models to take these returns as given. That is, they are considered to be draws of some exogenous random-number generator. Yet returns are based on prices. In particular, they involve the prices that will be set in tomorrow's markets. To understand how these prices are set, we need dynamic asset-pricing theory.

Dynamic asset-pricing theory builds on dynamic portfolio optimization, which itself is based on stochastic dynamic programming. The main mathematical technique that one uses to solve dynamic programming problems is the Bellman principle. We start out with a brief review of this principle. We will elaborate on a simplification in the optimality conditions that obtains in the portfolio optimization context. This simplification is of utmost importance in empirical analysis because it eliminates the need to solve for the key component of the Bellman principle, namely, the Bellman function.

At the heart of asset-pricing theory is the notion that portfolio optimizing agents meet in the marketplace, and that their demands interact to drive prices to an equilibrium. The theory then focuses on the properties of securities prices in the ensuing equilibrium. The predictions are very general and have been widely used in practical financial decision-making.

Although asset-pricing theory focuses on equilibrium, little attention has been paid to the question of how financial markets reach equilibrium. We shall refer to the latter throughout this book as the price discovery process. The chapter will end with a brief description of how one could go about modeling this process in a plausible and tractable way. The exercise leads to some interesting conclusions, opening up the way for much-needed further research.

1.2   Stochastic Dynamic Programming

We refrain from treating stochastic dynamic programming in its full generality. Instead, a specific problem is studied that encompasses most of the portfolio optimization problems that have been the basis of discrete-time, stationary dynamic asset-pricing models.

Let t index time: $t = 0, 1, 2, \ldots, T$. (In much of what follows, we take $T = \infty$.) There is an $M \times 1$ *state vector* x_t and a $K \times 1$ *control vector* y_t. The state vector x_t summarizes the state of the investor's environment: wealth, parameters of the distribution of returns (if these change over time), the riskfree rate (if a riskfree asset is available), the history of consumption, etc. The control vector y_t consists of investment decisions: how much does the investor choose to allocate to each available asset? We measure these quantities in dollars, so that the total amount allocated to all available assets is also our investor's gross investment, and consumption can be obtained from subtracting gross investment from wealth.

Our agent has a period-t-utility function denoted by $u_t(x_t, y_t)$, which we will assume to be time-invariant, so that we can drop the time subscript: $u(x_t, y_t)$. Notice that utility can be both a function of the state and the control variables. Because of our interpretation of state and control, this dual dependence is necessary even if utility is just a function of period consumption, because period consumption is not a separate control, but can be obtained by subtracting gross investment (the sum of the control variables) from wealth (one of the state variables), as we discussed in the previous paragraph.

The agent discounts future utility by using a subjective discount factor δ. We assume:

$$\delta \leq 1. \tag{1.1}$$

Let $N(\cdot)$ denote the discounted value of future utility:

$$N(x_0, x_1, \ldots; y_0, y_1, \ldots) = \sum_{t=0}^{T} \delta^t u(x_t, y_t). \tag{1.2}$$

The time-additivity seems restrictive, but the period-utility function $u(\cdot)$ depends on both the control and the state, and the latter may include the past history of consumption, so that period-utility may depend on past consumption, effectively linking utilities of different periods. This will be demonstrated later on, in the section on time nonseparable preferences.

R_{t+1} denotes the $N \times 1$ stochastic *shock vector*, with distribution function $F_t(R_{t+1}|x_t, y_t)$. The symbol R_{t+1} indicates how we interpret the shocks: they are the returns on the available assets (time $t+1$ prices plus dividends, divided by time t prices). We take the distribution function to be time-invariant, so that we can drop the time subscript: $F(R_{t+1}|x_t, y_t)$. This is without loss of generality: variation over time in any parameter of this distribution function can be captured by including the parameter in the state vector on which the distribution function still depends.

In portfolio optimization problems, the distribution of the shock will only be allowed to be a function of the state, and not of the control. In other words, we will not be able to control directly the distribution of the shock. Because the shock is interpreted as the securities returns, this restriction is effectively an assumption of *perfect competition:* the agent must take the distribution of returns as given. Thus, we will write $F(R_{t+1}|x_t)$. It may appear that our investor could impact the distribution of returns indirectly, through the effect of controls on wealth (one of the state variables). Later on, we will explicitly rule out such indirect control as well. In fact, this will lead to a vast simplification of the dynamic programming problem that our investor faces. Again, these restrictions are not ad hoc: they reflect the assumption of perfect competition.

The state moves ("transits") from one state to another by means of the following *state-transition equation*, which we also take to be time-invariant (hence we drop the time index):

$$x_{t+1} = g_t(x_t, y_t, R_{t+1})$$
$$= g(x_t, y_t, R_{t+1}).$$

Notice that the distribution of the future state x_{t+1}, conditional on the past state x_t and the control y_t, is induced by the (conditional) distribution of R_{t+1}. Wealth is one of the state variables; hence, one of the state transition equations will merely capture how wealth changes as a function of returns and investment choice.

We want to maximize the expected discounted value of future utility:

$$\max_{y_0, y_1, \ldots} E\left[N(x_0, x_1, \ldots; y_0, y_1, \ldots)|x_0\right]$$
$$= \max_{y_0, y_1, \ldots} E\left[\sum_{t=0}^{T} \delta^t u(x_t, y_t)|x_0\right].$$

Hopefully the solution will be simple. In particular, we hope that the optimal policy y_t is a function only of the contemporaneous state x_t: $y_t = h_t(x_t)$, in which case one refers to a *Markovian strategy*. It is not obvious that such an assumption is correct. In fact, it is not even obvious whether the optimal policy will be measurable in the states: the optimal policy may involve randomization. But if indeed $y_t = h_t(x_t)$, then our assumptions imply that the joint process of the state and the control is Markovian (i.e., that its distribution conditional on the past depends only on the immediate past).

It would distract too much from the main purpose of this book if we were to elaborate on the issue of whether the optimal policy is Markovian. The reader is warned that the answer may be negative, and is referred for further information to the excellent treatments in Bertsekas and Shreve (1976) and Lucas and Stokey (1989).

If it exists and is measurable in x_t, solving for the optimal policy y_t is facilitated by the Bellman principle, which states that there exists a sequence of functions of the state only, $V_t(x_t)$, $t = 0, 1, 2, \ldots$, called *value functions*, such that the optimal policies $y_0, y_1, y_2, \ldots$, can be obtained by recursively solving the following sequence of optimization problems:

$$V_t(x_t) = \max_y \left\{ u(x_t, y) + \delta E \left[V_{t+1} \left(g(x_t, y, R_{t+1}) \right) | x_t \right] \right\}. \qquad [1.3]$$

The reader should verify that our assumptions so far imply that the expectation of functions of future information (state, policy, shock) will indeed be a function of the immediate past state and policy only.

Let us study the first-order conditions for the problem in (1.3). For this to make sense, we must take u as well as V_t ($t = 0, 1, 2, \ldots$) to be continuously differentiable in their arguments. The former is a matter of assumption, the latter is not. Again, the issue would distract us here, but a discussion can be found in the aforementioned references.

The first-order conditions for control k are given in (1.4). Given x_t, the optimal strategy (point) is determined by:

$$\frac{\partial u(x_t, y)}{\partial y_k} + \delta E \left[\sum_{m=1}^{M} \frac{\partial V_{t+1}(g(x_t, y, R_{t+1}))}{\partial x_{m,t+1}} \frac{\partial g_m(x_t, y, R_{t+1})}{\partial y_k} | x_t \right] = 0. \qquad [1.4]$$

Varying x_t, we get a strategy function $y_t = h_t(x_t)$, which we hope is continuously differentiable. Again, this is not obvious, and must be proven.

Very often, it is indeed possible to prove that a continuously differentiable value function and Markovian strategies obtain, but computing them explicitly may be impossible. This certainly is annoying when we want to verify empirically an asset-pricing model that is based on dynamic portfolio optimization. Our inference error is already influenced by our ignorance of the key parameters that affect the distribution of the shocks (we may not even know this distribution at all, and have to rely on non-parametric procedures). We would like not to make things worse by introducing an additional error from numerical computation of the optimum portfolio strategies, if only because it is hard to control inference when the error is partly statistical (sampling error) and partly deterministic (numerical error).

Fortunately, dynamic portfolio-allocation problems generally lead to a simplification that effectively circumvents these issues. As a matter of fact, we will have to compute neither the optimal policies nor the Bellman functions when testing the asset-pricing model that they induce. This obtains because of natural restrictions on the state transition equation, which, like the restriction that the distribution of the shocks (returns) be independent of the controls, are motivated by assuming perfect competition.

To see what happens in the abstract stochastic dynamic control problem, consider the envelope condition at $t + 1$:

$$\frac{\partial V_{t+1}(x_{t+1})}{\partial x_{m,t+1}}$$

$$= \frac{\partial u(x_{t+1}, h_{t+1}(x_{t+1}))}{\partial x_{m,t+1}} + \delta E \left[\sum_{l=1}^{M} \frac{\partial V_{t+2}(g(x_{t+1}, h_{t+1}(x_{t+1}), R_{t+2}))}{\partial x_{l,t+2}} \times \right.$$

$$\left. \frac{\partial g_l(x_{t+1}, h_{t+1}(x_{t+1}), R_{t+2})}{\partial x_{m,t+1}} | x_{t+1} \right]$$

$$+ \delta \frac{\partial E[V_{t+2}(g(x_{t+1}, h_{t+1}(x_{t+1}), R_{t+2}))|x_{t+1}]}{\partial x_{m,t+1}}, \qquad [1.5]$$

where the last term has to be interpreted as the derivative of the expected Bellman function w.r.t. the conditioning variable x_{t+1}.

Now consider the case where:

1. The first state does not influence any of the state transition equations:

$$\frac{\partial g_l(x_{t+1}, h_{t+1}(x_{t+1}), R_{t+2})}{\partial x_{1,t+1}} = 0, \qquad [1.6]$$

where $l = 1, \ldots, M$;

2. Neither does it influence the distribution of the future shock:

$$\frac{\partial F(R_{t+2}|x_{t+1})}{\partial x_{1,t+1}} = 0, \qquad [1.7]$$

and hence,

$$\frac{\partial E[V_{t+2}(g(x_{t+1}, h_{t+1}(x_{t+1}), R_{t+2}))|x_{t+1}]}{\partial x_{1,t+1}} = 0;$$

3. None of the controls affects the state transition equations except for the first state:

$$\frac{\partial g_m}{\partial y_k} = 0, \qquad [1.8]$$

where $m = 2, \ldots, M$, $k = 1, \ldots, K$.

By interpreting the first state variable as wealth, these amount to assumptions of competitive behavior on the part of the agent. The first assumption states that the agent cannot indirectly control her environment (through the impact of investment decisions—controls—on her wealth), except, of course, for her own wealth (the first state variable). The second states that she cannot indirectly control the distribution of asset returns (shocks). The third assumption states that our investor cannot directly control her environment (state vector, except wealth) either.

Combining (1.5) and (1.4) then implies that the first-order conditions simplify to:

$$-\delta E \left[\frac{\frac{\partial u(x_{t+1}, h_{t+1}(x_{t+1}))}{\partial x_{1,t+1}}}{\frac{\partial u(x_t, y)}{\partial y_k}} \frac{\partial g_1(x_t, y, R_{t+1})}{\partial y_k} \Big| x_t \right] = 1. \qquad [1.9]$$

This is a remarkable simplification, because the first-order conditions do not directly involve the Bellman function. The result is quite surprising, because it says that the optimal control at t is entirely determined by the impact on the ratio of marginal utility at t and at $t+1$, given the optimal policy at $t+1$, as well as the effect on the state transition between t and $t+1$. It is unnecessary to account for effects on utility beyond $t+1$. In general, it is not sufficient to consider substitution effects between only t and $t+1$, because changes in the time t policy may influence utility far beyond $t+1$.

Because the expectation in (1.9) can be written as an integral, the equation is really an integral equation, which prompted economists to call it a *stochastic Euler equation*, a term borrowed from calculus of variation.

Economists insist on stationarity. That is, they would like the Bellman function and the optimal policies to be time-invariant functions of the state. This will be important in the empirical analysis, as explained in Chapter 2. Under stationarity, we can drop the time subscripts and merely refer to the beginning-of-period state and policy as x and y, respectively, and to the end-of-period state and policy as x' and y', respectively. Let R denote the period shock (return). The Bellman equation (1.3) becomes:

$$V(x) = \max_{y}\{u(x, y) + \delta E[V(g(x, y, R))|x]\}, \qquad [1.10]$$

and the first-order conditions are now:

$$\frac{\partial u(x, y)}{\partial y_k} + \delta E\left[\sum_{m=1}^{M} \frac{\partial V(g(x, y, R))}{\partial x_m'} \frac{\partial g_m(x, y, R)}{\partial y_k}\bigg| x\right] = 0. \quad [1.11]$$

The simplifying conditions are restated as follows.

1. The first state does not influence any of the state transition equations:

$$\frac{\partial g_l(x', h(x'), R')}{\partial x_1'} = 0,$$

where $l = 1, \ldots, M$;

2. Neither does it influence the distribution of the future shock:

$$\frac{\partial F(R'|x')}{\partial x_1'} = 0,$$

and hence,

$$\frac{\partial E[V(g(x, h(x), R))|x']}{\partial x_1'} = 0;$$

3. None of the controls affects the state transition equations except for the first state:

$$\frac{\partial g_m}{\partial y_k} = 0,$$

where $m = 2, \ldots, M, k = 1, \ldots, K$. The stochastic Euler equations then simplify to:

$$-\delta E\left[\frac{\frac{\partial u(x', h(x'))}{\partial x_1'}}{\frac{\partial u(x,y)}{\partial y_k}} \frac{\partial g_1(x, y, R)}{\partial y_k}\bigg| x\right] = 1. \qquad [1.12]$$

1.3   Application to a Simple Investment-Consumption Problem

Let us now translate the abstract results of the previous section into the concrete problem of the simplest portfolio investment problem: how much to consume and how much to invest? There is one good, which we refer to as the *dollar*. It can be either consumed or invested. In the latter case, it produces an uncertain return.

Although unorthodox, the most transparent translation defines the state and control (policy) variables as suggested in the previous section. In particular, let the first state variable x_1 be wealth (measured in terms of the single good) available for either consumption or investment at the beginning of the period (x_1' will be available at the beginning of the next period). We interpret the control as investment, and the shock as return. Because there is only one asset, $N = K = 1$. Therefore, the policy variable y is the remaining wealth at the beginning of the period, after consumption has been subtracted. The shock variable R is the return on the investment over the period. We impose the simplifying assumption (1.7): the distribution of R_t is independent of x_1. Since x_1 is the investor's wealth, the latter is really an assumption of competitive behavior, as already mentioned: the investor never has enough wealth to influence prices, and hence, the return distribution. The reader can immediately infer from this that the present model cannot be used to analyze investment choice in a strategic environment (e.g., a monopoly or oligopoly).

Our specification implies the following for the first transition equation:

$$x_1' = g_1(x, y, R) = yR.$$

We need specify neither the nature of the remaining state variables nor their transition equations. These state variables only influence the outcome through their effect on the conditional distribution of the return R. But we do assume that their state transition equations are unaffected by investment, either directly or indirectly—assumptions (1.6) and (1.8). This effectively means that our investor cannot influence her environment through her actions, except for her own wealth. Again, these are assumptions about competitive behavior.

Let the utility be logarithmic, that is:

$$u(x, y) = \ln(x_1 - y).$$

To facilitate cross-reference to established formulae in the literature, let c denote consumption. Consumption is what remains after investing wealth: $c = x_1 - y$. Define:

$$\bar{u}(c) = u(x, y).$$

Because we imposed (1.6)–(1.8), we can use the simplified first-order conditions in (1.12) to find the optimal consumption-investment policy (provided the outcome is stationary; otherwise, we have to refer to (1.9)). In this case, (1.12) reads:

$$\delta E\left[\frac{x_1 - y}{x_1' - y'}R|x\right] = 1.$$

Let us guess an optimal policy where investment is proportional to the beginning-of-period wealth, that is:

$$y = \gamma x_1. \tag{1.13}$$

Of course, for stationarity, we should guess $y' = \gamma x_1'$ as well. The reader can easily verify that this policy does indeed satisfy the first-order conditions, with $\gamma = \delta$. Writing this in terms of consumption:

$$c = (1 - \delta)x_1,$$

that is, our investor consumes a fixed fraction of her wealth.

In fact, we have obtained a well-known result, namely, that an investor with logarithmic preferences invests in a *myopic* way: her investment policy does not change with the state of the world, except for her own wealth. There can be substantial predictability in returns (through the state variables $x_2, \ldots, x_M$), but our investor keeps investing a fixed fraction of her wealth.

Notice that we did not have to solve for the Bellman function to find the optimal policy—a dramatic simplification of the problem.

1.4   A Nontrivial Portfolio Problem

We can readily extend the above to the case where there are multiple investment opportunities, called securities. The policy y is now a vector with N entries, namely, the number of dollars to be invested in each security. The return vector, R, has now N entries as well ($K = N$). The transition equation for the first state becomes:

$$x_1' = g_1(x, y, R) = \sum_{n=1}^{N} y_n R_n. \tag{1.14}$$

Because we shall need it in the next chapter, we will consider general one-period preferences. They are a function of consumption $c = x_1 - \sum_{n=1}^{N} y_n$ only:

$$\tilde{u}(c) = \tilde{u}(x_1 - \sum_{n=1}^{N} y_n) = u(x, y).$$

We make the same simplifying assumptions as in the previous section, and obtain the following stochastic Euler equations, written in terms of consumption. For $n = 1, \ldots, N$,

$$\delta E\left[\frac{\frac{\partial \tilde{u}(c')}{\partial c'}}{\frac{\partial \tilde{u}(c)}{\partial c}} R_n | x\right] = 1. \qquad [1.15]$$

That is, the optimal portfolio is such that the (conditional) expectation of the marginal rate of substitution of consumption times the return on each asset equals δ^{-1}.[2]

Equation (1.15) will be crucial to understanding asset-pricing theory.

1.5 Portfolio Separation

In the static (one-period) case, theorists observed early on that the optimal portfolio strategy often involved *portfolio separation*, which means that the optimal portfolio for a variety (or even all) of risk-averse preferences can be obtained as a simple portfolio of a number of basic portfolios, referred to as mutual funds (see Ross [1978]). This facilitated the development of asset-pricing models. In particular, it led to the CAPM of Sharpe (1964), Lintner (1965), and Mossin (1966).

Given its importance in empirical research, we should examine the static case. Although we have been working in a dynamic context, it is fairly easily adjusted to accommodate the static models by considering the last period, $T - 1$ to T. To simplify notation, let the primed variables (x', y') refer to time T, and those without a prime (x, y) refer to time $T - 1$. R denotes the return over $(T - 1, T)$.

---

2. The ratio of marginal utilities is traditionally referred to as the marginal rate of substitution. The term is suggested by the nonstochastic case, where the optimal rate of substitution of consumption over time or across goods is indeed given by the ratio of marginal utilities, as a consequence of the implicit function theorem. Any introductory textbook in economics establishes this relation.

At T, the investor consumes everything: $c' = x'_1$.

Consider *quadratic utility*:

$$\tilde{u}(c) = ac - \frac{b}{2}c^2,$$

where $a > 0$, $b > 0$. Marginal utility is a function of c:

$$\frac{\partial \tilde{u}(c)}{\partial c} = a - bc.$$

With quadratic utility, investors care only about the mean and variance of the return on their portfolio. For this reason, quadratic utility is often referred to as mean-variance preferences, and the optimal portfolio as the *mean-variance optimal*: it provides minimal return variance for its mean.

The optimality condition in (1.15) can be applied directly, producing:

$$\delta E[(a - bx'_1)R_n|x] = \lambda, \qquad [1.16]$$

where

$$\lambda = a - bc.$$

(The second-order condition for optimality holds, because $b > 0$.)

To show how portfolio separation works, split the payoff on the optimal portfolio ($\sum_{n=1}^{N} y_n R_n$, or, equivalently, x'_1) into (1) a riskfree part with return R_F (assuming it exists) and (2) a portfolio of risky securities *only*, with return R_b:

$$x'_1 = \eta_{F,x} R_F + \eta_{b,x} R_b,$$

where $\eta_{F,x}$ is the dollar amount invested in the riskfree security, and $\eta_{b,x}$ is the dollar amount invested in risky securities (these quantities can vary with x, whence the subscript). Let us refer to the portfolio of risky securities only as the *benchmark portfolio*.

Now project the excess return on security n onto that of the benchmark portfolio:

$$R_n - R_F = \alpha_{n,x} + \beta_{n,x}(R_b - R_F) + \epsilon_n. \qquad [1.17]$$

This is a conditional projection, which means that the error satisfies the following *conditional moment restrictions*:

$$E[\epsilon_n R_b|x] = E[\epsilon_n|x] = 0. \qquad [1.18]$$

The conditioning justifies the subscript x on the intercept and slope, α_n and β_n, respectively. If time-variant, the riskfree rate R_F will be one of the remaining state variables $x_2, \ldots, x_M$. Hence, (1.18) is equivalent to

$$E[\epsilon_n(R_b - R_F)|x] = E[\epsilon_n|x] = 0,$$

which is the usual definition of (conditional) projection.

Apply the optimality condition in (1.16) to R_n and R_F and take the difference:

$$\delta E[(a - bx_1')(R_n - R_F)|x] = 0. \qquad [1.19]$$

Next, apply (1.17):

$$\delta E[(a - bx_1')\alpha_{n,x}|x] + \delta \beta_{n,x} E[(a - bx_1')(R_b - R_F)|x]$$
$$+ \delta E[(a - bx_1')\epsilon_n|x] = 0. \qquad [1.20]$$

By construction (see (1.18)), the third term is zero:

$$E[(a - bx_1')\epsilon_n|x] = aE[\epsilon_n|x] - \eta_{F,x}R_F bE[\epsilon_n|x] - \eta_{b,x}bE[\epsilon_n R_b|x] = 0.$$

The second term is zero, by the assumption that x_1' is constructed optimally: (1.19) holds for each R_n, which means that it holds for any linear combination (portfolio) of returns, and, in particular, for R_b.

So, *if R_b is to provide the return on the risky part of the optimal portfolio, it is necessary that, for all n:*

$$\boxed{\alpha_{n,x} = 0.} \qquad [1.21]$$

When (1.21) holds, the first term in (1.20) will be zero as well, as required by optimality.

The condition in (1.21) is *sufficient* as well: it can be used to construct an optimal portfolio for any person with quadratic utility (i.e., any choice of a and b): first determine for which benchmark portfolio the return R_b is such that $\alpha_{n,x} = 0$, for all n. Next, choose the weights $\eta_{F,x}$ and $\eta_{b,x}$ such that the second term in (1.20) is zero. The third term will be zero by construction.

We have obtained *portfolio separation*: the optimal portfolio for investors with quadratic utility can be obtained as a linear combination of the riskfree security and a benchmark portfolio that is the same for everyone. This also means that all investors effectively demand the same portfolio of risky securities in the marketplace, a powerful result that can readily be exploited to get sharp asset-pricing results, as illustrated below.

It is interesting to work out the choice of $\eta_{b,x}$ that makes the resulting portfolio of the riskfree security and the benchmark portfolio optimal for a given investor. It is (the derivation is left as an exercise):

$$\eta_{b,x} = -\frac{E[R_b - R_F|x]}{\text{var}(R_b - R_F|x)} \frac{a - bE[x'_1|x]}{-b}. \qquad [1.22]$$

That is, the optimal choice is minus the product of the reward to risk ratio times the ratio of the expected marginal utility of future wealth over the change in this expected marginal utility. The implications are intuitive: as the coefficient of risk aversion, b, increases, $\eta_{b,x}$ decreases (provided the reward to risk ratio is positive). This means that a more risk-averse person puts fewer dollars into risky investments.

An important caveat is in order. Portfolio separation will obviously not obtain if investors hold differing beliefs about the distribution of returns and states, because they would each compute different expectations, variances, and covariances. Their portfolio demands would reflect these differences in beliefs, and hence, cannot necessarily be described in terms of demand for a riskfree security and a benchmark portfolio, even if they all have quadratic preferences.

Two final remarks:

1. There is a way to obtain portfolio separation for all types of risk-averse preferences, not just quadratic preferences. We merely have to turn the linear projection conditions in (1.18) into *conditional mean independence:*

$$E[\epsilon_n|R_b - R_F, x] = 0. \qquad [1.23]$$

(See Ross [1978].) In other words, the projection in (1.17) is a regression.[3] If returns are (conditionally) normally distributed,

---

3. There is a subtle but important distinction between linear projection and regression that is not always made clear in introductory textbooks of statistics or econometrics. Projection is a mere mathematical exercise that is always possible (except for pathological cases): one computes the intercept and slope in such a way that the error is uncorrelated (i.e., orthogonal) to the variable on the right-hand side of the equation (i.e., the explanatory variable). Regression, in contrast, is a statistical exercise. One determines the function of the explanatory variable that provides the expectation of the variable on the left-hand side (i.e., the dependent variable). It is rare that this function is linear. If it is, then the

linear projection and regression coincide, which means that we automatically obtain portfolio separation, no matter what the investors' preferences are. That normally distributed returns give portfolio separation will be demonstrated explicitly in the last section of this chapter.

2. The conditional mean independence restriction in (1.23) is restrictive and may hold only if two or more benchmark portfolios are considered simultaneously. That is, one may need K benchmark portfolios ($K \geq 2$) with returns $R_{b,k}$, such that the error in

$$R_n - R_F = \alpha_{n,x} + \sum_{k=1}^{K} \beta_{k,n,x}(R_{b,k} - R_F) + \epsilon_n$$

satisfies the conditional mean independence restriction

$$E[\epsilon_n | R_{b,k} - R_F, k = 1, \ldots, K; x] = 0.$$

If so, we will obtain $K + 1$-fund portfolio separation: K benchmark portfolios will be needed to reconstruct an investor's optimal portfolio, in addition to the riskfree security.

1.6 Toward the First Asset-Pricing Model

Having explored portfolio choice, we are now ready to establish our first asset-pricing result. We already hinted at it in the previous section.

Let us assume that two-fund portfolio separation holds, that is, investors' optimal portfolios can be decomposed into a riskfree security and a benchmark portfolio of risky securities only. This would obtain if all investors use quadratic utility, or if returns on risky securities are jointly normally distributed. We also assume that investors hold common beliefs. The situation is thus vastly simplified: all investors demand the same portfolio of risky securities (the benchmark portfolio). This demand meets the supply in the marketplace. The supply of risky securities is called the *market portfolio*. For the market to be in equilibrium (i.e., for demand

---

coefficients can be found by projection, and the error will not only be uncorrelated with the explanatory variable, but also mean-independent. This means that the assumption of a linear regression function is a restriction on the data. A quite severe one, for that matter, but it does obtain when the explanatory and independent variables are jointly normal.

to match the supply) the market portfolio and the benchmark portfolio must coincide.

This implies, in particular, that *the market portfolio must be an optimal portfolio*, which means that it satisfies the same restrictions as the benchmark portfolio, namely, (1.21). Let R_M denote the return on the market portfolio. Project the excess return on all the assets onto that of the market portfolio:

$$R_n - R_F = \alpha_{n,x}^M + \beta_{n,x}^M (R_M - R_F) + \epsilon_n^M. \qquad [1.24]$$

The error will have the following properties:

$$E[\epsilon_n^M R_M | x] = E[\epsilon_n^M | x] = 0.$$

In equilibrium:

$$\alpha_{n,x}^M = 0, \qquad [1.25]$$

for all n.

This asset-pricing model has become known as the CAPM and was first derived by Sharpe (1964), Lintner (1965), and Mossin (1966). Taking expectations in (1.24), we can rewrite the condition in (1.25) in a more familiar form. For all n:

$$\boxed{E[R_n - R_F | x] = \beta_{n,x}^M E[R_M - R_F | x].} \qquad [1.26]$$

That is, the expected excess return on a security is proportional to its risk, as measured by the projection coefficient . The projection coefficient has become known as the security's *beta*.

There are two important remarks to be made about the developments so far. First, at the core of the CAPM is the notion of equilibrium. That is, the predictions that the theory makes about prices in a financial market rely on the belief that these markets somehow equilibrate. There is a school of thought in economics, the Neo-Austrian school, that rejects the very idea that markets equilibrate. We demonstrate later that equilibration, or *price discovery*, as we call it, is indeed far from a foregone conclusion.

Second, although (1.26) is referred to as an asset-pricing model, prices do not enter explicitly. They only enter implicitly, in that the return equals tomorrow's payoff divided by today's price. Equilibration, then, requires that the market search for the prices such that the return distributions for all the securities satisfy (1.26). There is an issue as to whether there exist prices such that (1.26) can hold at all. That is, *equilibrium existence* is not a foregone conclusion. We will postpone discussion until the end of this chapter.

1.7 Consumption-Based Asset-Pricing Models

The argument that led to the asset-pricing model in the previous section is based on identification of a portfolio that must be optimal in equilibrium. A variation of this argument is to identify a consumption process that must be optimal in equilibrium. Let us investigate this now.

We again start with the first-order conditions, this time expressed directly in terms of consumption, namely 1.15:

$$\delta E \left[\frac{\frac{\partial \bar{u}(c')}{\partial c'}}{\frac{\partial \bar{u}(c)}{\partial c}} R_n | x \right] = 1. \qquad [1.27]$$

This is a restriction at the individual level, prescribing how individual consumption must correlate with asset returns to be optimal. It is silent about market-wide phenomena, in particular, equilibrium.

It does become an equilibrium restriction, however, if it holds for *all* investors, that is, if all investors implement a consumption-investment policy that is optimal, and hence, satisfies (1.27).

It is hard to test such a proposition, for lack of data on individual consumption. One would like to work with aggregate data, which are more readily available. In particular, a restriction in terms of aggregate consumption is desirable.

We immediately conclude that if all investors are alike, aggregate consumption (both preferences and beliefs) must be optimal as well, for in that case, aggregate and private consumption are perfectly correlated (i.e., in equilibrium).

We thus obtain Lucas' consumption-based asset pricing model (Lucas [1978]), which states that the aggregate consumption at the beginning and end of each period, c_A and c'_A, respectively, must be such that

$$\delta E \left[\frac{\frac{\partial \bar{u}(c'_A)}{\partial c'}}{\frac{\partial \bar{u}(c_A)}{\partial c}} R_n | x \right] = 1, \qquad [1.28]$$

for all n.

The assumption of identical investors is objectionable, but can readily be relaxed in two ways:

1. One could assume that financial markets are *complete*, which means that there are an equal number of securities and possible outcomes. This is equivalent to saying that all risk can be insured (even if not necessarily at a fair price). Arrow (1953) and Debreu (1959) have shown that in such a case: (i) markets equilibrate; and (ii) the equilibrium consumption processes are Pareto optimal, in the sense that they solve a dynamic economy-wide consumption-investment problem as in (1.3), with respect to a social welfare function that is of the same form. In other words, there exists a representative agent whose preferences are described by this social welfare function, and who finds the aggregate consumption process to be optimal given the returns provided in the financial markets. The asset-pricing restriction (1.28) would then hold for aggregate consumption (see also Constantinides [1982]).[4]

2. One could restrict attention to preferences that can be "aggregated," in the sense that aggregate consumption and investment demands are as if determined by some aggregate investor. The idea is analogous to that of portfolio separation, where every investor essentially demands the same portfolio(s) of risky securities, but it extends to consumption as well. In this case, (1.28) should hold for aggregate consumption; otherwise the market is not in equilibrium (some investor, and hence, the aggregate investor, was not able to implement optimal consumption-investment plans). See Rubinstein (1974) for a list of preferences for which aggregation obtains.

It would distract us to elaborate on the technical aspects of either of the above relaxations on the assumption of identical investors. The interested reader should consult the references.

---

4. There seems to be little appreciation in the literature that this argument is problematic, because the welfare function will generally not be state-independent (as u in (1.28) is). The welfare function is really a weighted average of the utility function of all the agents in the economy, with the weights determined by marginal utility of wealth. Hence, the weights depend on the distribution of wealth, and the welfare function will as well. That is, the welfare function depends on state variables that capture the distribution of wealth.

The consumption-based model in (1.28) has the advantage that it is dynamic, in contrast to the CAPM, which is static. But the CAPM has the advantage that it provides equilibrium restrictions in terms of financial market data only. Instead, the consumption-based model is cast in terms of aggregate consumption. Although aggregate consumption data are available, they may not be as reliable as pure financial data. The frequent revision of older aggregate consumption statistics demonstrates their unreliability.

Rubinstein (1976) has derived a simple dynamic asset-pricing model, where he managed to substitute the market portfolio for aggregate consumption. We cover it in some detail here, because it features prominently in later chapters, both theoretically and empirically. (Rubinstein derived more general versions of the model than we discuss here; we focus on the simplest one, because of its pedagogical merits.)

We assume that investors are all alike (beliefs and preferences), and that they have logarithmic preferences, as in Section 1.3. In this case, optimal aggregate consumption is a fixed fraction of aggregate wealth. Letting x_A and x_A' denote aggregate wealth at the beginning and end of the period, respectively, this means:

$$c_A = (1 - \delta)x_A$$

and

$$c_A' = (1 - \delta)x_A'.$$

What is the future aggregate wealth? From the transition equation in (1.14), we can infer that it is determined by the payoff on the shares that the aggregate investor demands:

$$x_A' = \sum_{n=1}^{N} y_{A,n} R_n,$$

where $y_{A,n}$ denotes the aggregate demand for security n. At the same time, today's aggregate wealth equals the total amount invested (i.e., δx_A). Hence, the total *return* that is demanded equals $x_A'/(\delta x_A)$.

For the market to be in equilibrium, this demanded return must equal the total return available in the marketplace. Hence, it must be the return on the market portfolio, *if* we allow it to include the riskfree security (which we did not permit in the previous section). This implies:

$$\frac{x'_A}{\delta x_A} = R_M.$$

Plugging this in (1.28) generates the following equilibrium restrictions:

$$E\left[\frac{\delta x_A}{x'_A} R_n | x\right] = \boxed{E\left[\frac{1}{R_M} R_n | x\right] = 1,} \qquad [1.29]$$

for all n. We will refer to this set of restrictions as Rubinstein's model.

There is a close relationship between the CAPM and Rubinstein's model, not surprisingly. A few additional assumptions bring us very close, but there is an important difference, which justifies paying some attention to the difference between CAPM and Rubinstein's model.

Assume, in particular, that R_M is conditionally lognormal with $E[\ln R_M | x] = \mu_{M,x}$, $\mathrm{var}(\ln R_M | x) = \sigma^2_{M,x}$. Likewise, some individual asset returns are lognormal, say, assets $n = 1, \ldots, N_1$, with $E[\ln R_n | x] = \mu_{n,x}$, $\mathrm{var}(\ln R_n | x) = \sigma^2_{n,x}$. Not all assets can be lognormal, because the market portfolio is a linear combination of all the assets, and could not have a lognormally distributed return, because linear combinations of lognormal random variables are not lognormal.

The correlation between $\ln R_M$ and $\ln R_n$ ($n = 1, \ldots, N_1$) is ρ_n.

Tedious algebra (see the Exercises) reveals the following:

$$\mu_{n,x} - \ln R_F = 2\tilde{\beta}^M_{x,n}(\mu_{M,x} - \ln R_F) - \tfrac{1}{2}\sigma^2_{n,x}. \qquad [1.30]$$

The risk measure is:

$$\tilde{\beta}^M_{x,n} = \frac{\mathrm{cov}(\ln R_n, \ln R_M | x)}{\mathrm{var}(\ln R_M | x)}.$$

The correction term $-\tfrac{1}{2}\sigma^2_{n,x}$ is typical when lognormal random variables are transformed by the logarithmic function.

(1.30) is almost the CAPM; compare to (1.26). But the restriction obtains only for log returns, and even then is not formally the same. In particular, the market portfolio will not be optimal for an investor using quadratic utility (i.e., it will not be mean-variance optimal). But it is optimal for logarithmic preferences.

This version of Rubinstein's model also makes an interesting prediction about the expected log return of the market portfolio. As an exercise, the reader is asked to prove that:

$$\mu_{M,x} - \ln R_F = \sigma_{M,x}^2 - \tfrac{1}{2}\sigma_{M,x}^2. \qquad [1.31]$$

(The term $-\tfrac{1}{2}\sigma_{M,x}^2$ is deliberately kept separate, because it is a standard correction for lognormal random variables.) That is, the average logarithmic return in excess of the log return on the riskfree asset is proportional to the asset's conditional variance. Hence, the risk premium on the market portfolio is determined by its variance. The higher the variance, the higher the marketwide risk premium. This implication is similar to the one found in Merton (1980) (which presents a continuous-time model).

1.8   Asset-Pricing Theory: The Bottom Line

Let us try to distill the common prediction of the asset-pricing models we have been studying. They all originate in the stochastic Euler equations of (1.15), and state that

$$E[AR_n|x] = 1, \qquad [1.32]$$

where A measures aggregate risk. In the CAPM, A is a linear transformation of the return on the market portfolio. In Lucas' consumption-based model, A is the marginal rate of substitution of consumption in the beginning and end of a period. In the Rubinstein model, it equals the inverse return on the market portfolio, that is,

$$A = \frac{1}{R_M}. \qquad [1.33]$$

We can express (1.32) in terms of covariances. Because it is always true that for two random variables Y and Z, $E[YZ|x] = \text{cov}(Y, Z|x) + E[Y|x]E[Z|x]$, we can restate (1.32) as follows:

$$\boxed{E[R_n|x] - R_F = -\text{cov}\left(\frac{A}{E[A|x]}, R_n|x\right).} \qquad [1.34]$$

That is, mean excess returns are proportional to the covariance with aggregate risk.

Equation (1.34), then, is the central prediction of asset-pricing theory.

1.9 Arrow-Debreu Securities Pricing

It was mentioned before that one version of Lucas' model is the complete-markets model of Arrow (1953) and Debreu (1959).[5] In it, a particular type of security plays an important role, namely, the *Arrow-Debreu security*, referred to as AD security. It pays one dollar in one state, and zero in all others. It may not be traded literally, but can be obtained by a portfolio of traded securities.

Consider two end-of-period states w and v. Let the beginning-of-period price of AD security w be $P_{x,w}$. Let $P_{x,v}$ denote the beginning-of-period price of AD security v. The return on the former, R_w, equals:

$$R_w = \begin{cases} \frac{1}{P_{x,w}} & \text{if state } w \text{ occurs,} \\ 0 & \text{otherwise.} \end{cases}$$

Likewise,

$$R_v = \begin{cases} \frac{1}{P_{x,v}} & \text{if state } v \text{ occurs,} \\ 0 & \text{otherwise.} \end{cases}$$

Let $\pi_{x,w}$ and $\pi_{x,v}$ denote the conditional probabilities of state w and v, respectively.

Apply Lucas' model (1.28) to obtain:

$$P_{x,w} = \delta \pi_{x,w} \frac{\frac{\partial \tilde{u}(c'_{A,w})}{\partial c'}}{\frac{\partial \tilde{u}(c_A)}{\partial c}},$$

where $c'_{A,w}$ denotes the aggregate end-of-period consumption in state w. Likewise,

$$P_{x,v} = \delta \pi_{x,v} \frac{\frac{\partial \tilde{u}(c'_{A,v})}{\partial c'}}{\frac{\partial \tilde{u}(c_A)}{\partial c}}.$$

Assume states w and v are equally likely (i.e., $\pi_{x,w} = \pi_{x,v}$). Taking the ratio of the two state prices produces:

5. The two models are not nested: Lucas' model is stationary, whereas Arrow and Debreu's model obtains in a nonstationary world as well; Lucas' model may obtain in an incomplete market (i.e., a market where not all risk can be insured); the Arrow-Debreu model requires completeness. Most importantly, the Arrow-Debreu model does not require that investors hold common beliefs; they may disagree, but not to the point that one investor thinks a state is impossible whereas another one thinks that it is possible.

$$\frac{P_{x,w}}{P_{x,v}} = \frac{\frac{\partial \bar{u}(c'_{A,w})}{\partial c'}}{\frac{\partial \bar{u}(c'_{A,v})}{\partial c'}}. \qquad [1.35]$$

That is, the ratio of the AD securities prices for two equally likely states is given by the ratio of the marginal utilities of aggregate consumption.

This has an important implication. Because marginal utility is decreasing (reflecting risk aversion), states with lower aggregate consumption will command a higher price . Loosely speaking, insurance for states with low aggregate consumption is relatively expensive.

1.10   Roll's Critique

The CAPM as well as Rubinstein's model are examples of a class of models that we could best describe as *portfolio-based asset-pricing models*. They identify a particular portfolio that must be optimal for the market to be in equilibrium. In both models, the market portfolio must be optimal. In the CAPM, the market portfolio is mean-variance optimal, and includes only risky assets. In Rubinstein's model, the market portfolio is optimal for logarithmic preferences, and must include the supply of riskfree securities.

If we cannot observe the portfolio that portfolio-based asset-pricing models predict to be optimal, the theory is without empirical content. Using a proxy portfolio will not do. For an optimal portfolio always exists (absent arbitrage opportunities), and hence, we could by chance choose a proxy that happened to be optimal (i.e., that satisfies the restrictions of asset-pricing theory).

This is the core argument of the *Roll critique* (Roll [1977]). In the context of the CAPM, Roll demonstrated that high correlation between the return on the proxy and the market portfolio is no indication that there is much to be learned from the properties of the proxy about the mean-variance optimality of the market portfolio.

In particular, let us suppose that, for some benchmark portfolio with return R_b, we find that $\alpha_{n,x} = 0$ for all n in

$$R_n - R_F = \alpha_{n,x} + \beta_{n,x}(R_b - R_F) + \epsilon_n.$$

This is not a test of the CAPM, but only an indication that the benchmark portfolio is mean-variance optimal. At best, it is a test that no arbitrage opportunities exist, for otherwise there would not be a mean-variance optimal portfolio.

The existence of such a portfolio can be exploited, however, to summarize the data. If we can find a benchmark portfolio (or combination of benchmark portfolios) that is mean-variance optimal, we can use a security's beta to determine its expected excess return:

$$E[R_n - R_F|x] = \beta_{n,x}E[R_b - R_F|x]. \qquad [1.36]$$

If the same portfolio (or set of portfolios) is found to be optimal across markets and over time, we conclude that there is a regularity in the data that can be used to predict expected excess returns in the future or in cross-section. Again, this is not evidence that financial markets equilibrate according to asset-pricing theory, but it is an interesting empirical fact that provides useful summary information about how markets price securities.

One wonders whether this is how recent work in empirical asset pricing has to be interpreted, because benchmark portfolios are being used that bear little relationship with the theory, and yet are found to be mean-variance optimal. The prototype is Fama and French (1996); a recent survey is Cochrane (1999). When multiple benchmark portfolios are found to explain the cross-section of expected excess returns, the outcome is called a *multifactor asset-pricing model*. This term is objectionable: unless there is a theoretical reason why the factor portfolios "work," it should not be referred to as an asset-pricing model.

1.11   Time Nonseparable Preferences

Early in this chapter, it was mentioned that our framework could accommodate time nonseparabilities, even if, from (1.2), our preferences look purely separable. In particular, we can make utility depend on past consumption levels.

Consider the following utility function, evaluated at a state and control of the future (variables with a prime):

$$u(x', y') = \frac{(x'_1 - y' + \lambda x'_s)^{\gamma+1}}{\gamma + 1},$$ [1.37]

where x'_1 denotes future wealth before consumption (as before), y' denotes future wealth after consumption (the control), and x'_s is a new state variable with transition equation:

$$x'_s = x_1 - y;$$

λ is a parameter. Effectively, future-period utility is a function of (1) future consumption $x'_1 - y'$, and (2) prior-period consumption $x_1 - y$. This is a simple way of overcoming time separability in standard preferences. When $\lambda < 0$, consumption is intertemporally complementary, and one refers to this situation as habit persistence. A continuous-time version of this class of preferences was studied, among others, in Constantinides (1990) and Sundaresan (1989).

To simplify notation, let

$$z = x_1 - y + \lambda x_s.$$

The future equivalent carries a prime:

$$z' = x'_1 - y' + \lambda x'_s.$$

We use double primes when referring to two periods in the future:

$$z'' = x''_1 - y'' + \lambda x''_s.$$

As an exercise, the reader is asked to write down the resulting Bellman function for a standard portfolio problem, derive the first-order conditions, and to use the envelope condition to conclude that, for optimality,

$$- z^\gamma + \delta E\left[\left((z')^\gamma + \delta\lambda E[(z'')^\gamma | x'] \right) R_n | x \right] - \delta E[\lambda(z')^\gamma | x] = 0. \quad [*]$$

Under Lucas' assumption of a representative agent, these optimality conditions generate the following asset-pricing model. We will use the subscript A to indicate aggregate variables (i.e., those based on aggregate consumption):

$$E[AR_n | x] = 1,$$

with

$$A = \delta \frac{(z'_A)^\gamma + \delta\lambda E[(z''_A)^\gamma | x']}{z_A^\gamma + \delta\lambda E[(z'_A)^\gamma | x]}.$$

[1.38]

1.12   Existence of Equilibrium

We defined equilibrium in a rather casual way as a restriction on moments of the joint distribution of return and aggregate risk (see (1.34)) such that demand for securities equals their supply. But, in the context of the CAPM, we already hinted that existence of equilibrium and equilibration (price discovery) are not foregone conclusions, and hence, deserve some attention. We will first discuss existence of equilibrium.

One difficulty with proving existence of equilibrium is that prices are only implicit in the asset-pricing restrictions. In fact, returns are non-linear functions of beginning-of-period prices, so that a set of prices may not exist such that (1.34) holds.

There is a graver difficulty. In a dynamic context, end-of-period pay-offs are the sum of dividends plus the prices at the beginning of the next period, and hence, are endogenous to the model. We can take prices at the beginning of the next period to be equilibrium prices, but we do have to formulate how investors form beliefs about the distribution of future prices, or at least hypothesize what these beliefs are.

This issue did not come up in the complete-markets world of Arrow and Debreu. In it, all risks are supposed to be insurable at all times. Thus all possibilities are already priced at time zero by means of a straightforward Walrasian equilibrium,[6] and investors can simply read the future pricing of risks in the pattern of prices of AD securities with different maturities (see Debreu [1959]).

In the general context, the standard solution due to Radner makes a stronger assumption about agents' predictive capabilities. It is hypothesized that investors can list tomorrow's states, and, for each state, write down what securities prices would be. In this case the investors know the

---

6. A Walrasian equilibrium is defined to be the set of prices such that, if investors submit their securities demands for those prices, total demand equals total supply.

mapping from states to prices. This hypothesis has become known as *rational expectations* (RE; see Radner [1972]).

In part, RE originates in the reasonable assumption that investors should be at least as good as the average economist, and hence, should be capable of working out equilibrium prices in any given state. The latter was first suggested by Muth (1961). But to work out equilibrium prices in future states requires an enormous amount of structural knowledge about the economy that even the best economist does not have.

It will be important for the remainder of this book that the reader distinguish between RE and unbiased predictions. To have RE merely makes the strong assumption that investors know what prices would obtain in each possible state. The beliefs that they hold about the chances that each state occurs may still be wrong, and hence, investors make biased forecasts. It should be equally clear, however, that RE and the assumption of unbiased predictions are not entirely unrelated.

Many do not distinguish between RE and unbiased predictions, assuming that investors know the future distribution of prices, effectively stating that they know: (1) the mapping from states to prices; and (2) the distribution of states. In other words, investors' beliefs are right. The assumption is motivated by the concern that stationarity of equilibrium return distributions will not obtain if investors' beliefs can be wrong. If investors realize that they are wrong, they learn, and hence, the state vector (x_t) should include their beliefs. Hopefully, beliefs converge. If so, the state vector does not constitute a stationary (i.e., time-invariant) process. Yet, stationarity facilitates empirical research, as will be discussed in the next chapter.

Even if investors' beliefs are correct, the existence of stationary equilibria is not a foregone conclusion. By correct beliefs we mean that the probability measure with which investors assess uncertainty coincides with the probability measure with which states are factually drawn. This is the assumption that Lucas made in deriving his asset-pricing model, discussed in earlier sections. Lucas referred to it as rational expectations, but, to distinguish it from Radner's notion, we will refer to it as *Lucas-RE*.

To study the existence of equilibrium in Lucas' framework, we obviously cannot work with returns, and must write the equilibrium restrictions explicitly in terms of prices. This also means, among other things, that the stochastic shocks now cannot be identified as returns. Instead, only the dividends that enter the return can be considered as shocks. Let D'_n denote the end-of-period dividend of security n.[7] D'_n will be the nth shock. The existence of equilibrium becomes a question of the existence of a *fixed point* in a mapping, as is now shown.

Decompose the return into prices and dividends:

$$R_n = \frac{P'_n + D'_n}{P_n}.$$

The question is: does there exist a function ϕ_n mapping the state into the positive part of the real line, such that:

$$P'_n = \phi_n(x'),$$

$$P_n = \phi_n(x),$$

and the equilibrium condition (1.28) holds? Equivalently, does there exist a mapping ϕ such that:

$$\delta E \left[\frac{\frac{\partial \tilde{u}(c'_A)}{\partial c'}}{\frac{\partial \tilde{u}(c_A)}{\partial c}} (\phi_n(x') + D_n) | x \right] = \phi_n(x), \qquad [1.39]$$

for all n. In more abstract notation: does there exist a fixed point[8] to the function G, mapping functions into functions, where:

$$G(\phi_n)(\cdot) = \delta E \left[\frac{\frac{\partial \tilde{u}(c'_A)}{\partial c'}}{\frac{\partial \tilde{u}(c_A)}{\partial c}} (\phi_n(x') + D_n) | \cdot \right]?$$

Under particular assumptions, Lucas demonstrates that the answer is affirmative. This is comforting, because it means that our asset-pricing theory makes sense after all.

1.13   Price Discovery

In addition to the existence of equilibrium, one wonders how financial markets equilibrate. In general equilibrium theory, this question has traditionally been cast in terms of the *stability* of equilibrium: if an economy is kicked off its equilibrium, will it return to it? There is an extensive literature on this in the context of the Arrow-Debreu model (see, e.g., Negishi

---

7. We could also insist that the dividends add up to the end-of-period consumption ($\sum_{n=1}^{N} D'_n = c'_A$), but this is not necessary.

8. The fixed point is the value ϕ_n such that $G(\phi_n)(x) = \phi_n(x)$, for all x.

[1962], Arrow and Hahn [1971]). But we have just concluded that our asset-pricing models require a more sophisticated notion of equilibrium than the Walrasian equilibrium that is used in Arrow and Debreu's world, namely, RE.

Most of the analysis to date has focused on how a market would learn the mapping from states to prices that is a crucial component of the RE equilibrium. Nice examples are Jordan (1985) and Marcet and Sargent (1989). Little attention is paid, however, to the question of how financial markets equilibrate given that this mapping is known, perhaps because the analyses are done using static models.

We will see that there may be problems here even within a simple CAPM example.

We need a model of price discovery. We have been assuming competitive behavior so far (i.e., investors cannot control their environment beyond their own consumption and investment policies). We will continue to make the assumption, rather than delve into strategic (i.e., game-theoretic) models of price discovery. Game-theoretic models have become popular in an area referred to as market microstructure theory.[9]

The prototype *competitive price-discovery model* is the Walrasian *tatonnement*. An auctioneer calls out a set of prices for all securities, investors reveal their demand at these prices, and the auctioneer collects the demands. If the total excess demand for a security is nonzero, the auctioneer calls out new prices, and a new round of demand revelation starts. The process stops if all markets clear. In the adjustment between rounds, the auctioneer could simply change the price of a security in the direc-

---

9. Market microstructure models, starting with Kyle (1985) and Glosten and Milgrom (1985), study how a market discovers an asset's "liquidation value," and hence, can also be considered equilibrium price-discovery models if the liquidation value is interpreted as equilibrium price. But these models are also equilibrium models, and beg the question of how their equilibrium is discovered. That is, the issue of equilibration is pushed back just one step. Many other aspects of market microstructure models make them less obvious candidates as models of price discovery of the equilibria in asset-pricing theory: because they are game-theoretic, market microstructure models make far stronger assumptions about common knowledge; categorization of traders into the classes of market makers, noise traders, and discretionary liquidity traders is absent from asset-pricing theory; risk neutrality is often assumed, whereas risk aversion is at the core of asset-pricing theory; etc. Finally, most market microstructure models focus on information aggregation—an issue that is largely ignored in the asset-pricing theory that has been used to explain historical data.

tion of the excess demand: if it is negative, raise the price; if it is positive, lower the price. We will use this simple adjustment process.

In the standard tatonnement process, there is no trade until all markets clear. A more realistic model of price discovery would have trade take place in each market, perhaps by randomly assigning demand to the suppliers when excess demand is positive, or randomly assigning supply to demanders when excess demand is negative. Models of price discovery with intermediate trading are referred to as *nontatonnement*. In the simple CAPM example given below, however, intermediate trading will be shown not to affect the evolution of prices. Hence, the distinction between tatonnement and nontatonnement is inconsequential as far as the evolution of prices is concerned.

The tatonnement process need not be taken literally, of course. There need not be an auctioneer, no rounds, etc. The mathematics will reflect only the essential parts: (1) investors cannot affect the adjustment process (competition); (2) adjustment works through prices, with prices changing as a function of demand pressure. Everything else is immaterial.

To focus on price discovery, we will concentrate on the static (one-period) case, which means that investors consume their entire end-of-period wealth. In addition, we will exclude consumption in the beginning of the period. This way, the model will be ready to be used to analyze some of the experimental results we will talk about in Chapter 4.

With the exception of the previous section, we have been working with returns rather than prices. An analysis of price discovery, however, requires that one explicitly state the problem in terms of prices. This means that we will have to redefine a few variables. We will also drop unnecessary conditioning, which would clutter the notation. Hence, the state variable x will be one-dimensional, and measure only an investor's wealth. On the other hand, we will have to explicitly consider differences among investors. We will introduce the index j to identify Q types of investors, distinguishable in terms of their risk aversion: $j = 1, \ldots, Q$. (It will not be necessary to distinguish investors according to their wealth, because we are going to assume constant absolute risk aversion.)

We will generate the CAPM here by assuming normally distributed returns. In this case, preferences trade-off means against variance (the only two parameters in the normal distribution). Moreover, we will assume constant absolute risk aversion, which implies that the trade-off between mean and variance will be independent of wealth.

As before, we will assume that a riskfree security exists. To facilitate notation, however, we will count $N + 1$ securities, the first one (security $n = 0$) being the riskfree security, and the remaining securities, $n = 1, \ldots, N$, being risky.

The price of the riskfree security will be used as numeraire at the beginning of the period, and it is assumed to pay one dollar at the end of the period. Investor j demands h_j units of the riskfree security. In terms of the earlier notation (with the addition of the subscript j, to identify the investor):

$$y_{j,0} = h_j.$$

Investor j demands $z_{j,n}$ units of each of the N risky securities. Security n carries a price of P_n. The latter is a normalized price, expressed in terms of the price of the riskfree security (rather than beginning-of-period dollars). Hence, in terms of the earlier notation:

$$y_{j,n} = z_{j,n} P_n,$$

where $n = 1, \ldots, N$.

It will be easier to switch to vector notation. In particular, let z_j denote the vector of units of the risky securities that investor j demands: $z_j = [z_{j,n}]_{n=1,\ldots,N}$. Similarly, let P denote the vector of the beginning-of-period prices of the n risky securities: $P = [P_n]_{n=1,\ldots,N}$.

Let D_n denote the dollar payoff of security n at the end of the period. From what we said before, $D_0 = 1$. For the risky securities, let D denote the vector of their payoffs ($D = [D_n]_{n=1,\ldots,N}$). Let μ denote the vector of expected payoffs ($\mu = [\mu_n]_{n=1,\ldots,N}$) and let Σ denote the covariance matrix,

$$\Sigma = [\text{cov}(D_w, D_v)]_{w=1,\ldots,N; v=1,\ldots,N}.$$

We assume that all investors agree on the means, variances, and covariances (i.e., beliefs are homogeneous).

Investor j's end-of-period utility, $\hat{u}_j$, will be a function only of h_j and z_j. In particular,

$$\hat{u}_j(h_j, z_j) = h_j + z_j^T \mu - \frac{b_j}{2} z_j^T \Sigma z_j, \qquad [1.40]$$

where T denotes transpose. The parameter b_j measures investor j's risk aversion (trade-off between mean and variance). It is assumed to be independent of wealth (i.e., the investor has constant absolute risk aversion).

At the beginning of the period there is no consumption, but investor j is endowed with a certain number h_j^0 of riskfree securities, and a vector z_j^0 of risky securities. Therefore, her budget constraint becomes:

$$h_j + P^T z_j = h_j^0 + P^T z_j^0. \qquad [1.41]$$

We can ignore discounting, because this is a static model.

Standard maximization of the utility (1.40) subject to the budget constraint in (1.41) generates the following first-order conditions:

$$z_j = \frac{1}{b_j} \Sigma^{-1} (\mu - \lambda_j P),$$

where λ_j is the Lagrange multiplier, which equals 1, from the first-order condition of the demand for the riskfree security. This means:

$$z_j = \frac{1}{b_j} \Sigma^{-1} (\mu - P). \qquad [1.42]$$

Incidentally, notice that we have here an example of portfolio separation. In (1.42), only the scalar b_j is specific to an individual. That is, up to a scaling constant, demand for risky securities is the same for everybody, namely,

$$\Sigma^{-1} (\mu - P).$$

The latter can be written as the *weights of a benchmark portfolio*, by normalization:

$$\Sigma^{-1} (\mu - P) / \hat{1}^T \Sigma^{-1} (\mu - P),$$

where $\hat{1}$ denotes a vector of ones.

With an equal number of investors of each type, total excess demand is just the sum of $h_j - h_j^0$ (riskfree security) and $z_j - z_j^0$ (risky securities). In equilibrium, prices must be such that:

$$\sum_{j=1}^{Q} (h_j - h_j^0) = 0,$$

and

$$\sum_{j=1}^{Q} (z_j - z_j^0) = 0.$$

The latter can be solved for prices (the former will then automatically be satisfied), which generates:

$$P = \mu - \frac{1}{\sum_{j=1}^{Q} \frac{1}{b_j}} \Sigma z^0, \qquad [1.43]$$

where z^0 denotes the vector of total initial holdings, that is,

$$z^0 = \sum_{j=1}^{Q} z_j^0.$$

Although it may not be immediately clear, the equilibrium in (1.43) is the CAPM. (In an exercise, the reader is asked to verify the link between (1.43) and (1.26).) As an aside, note that existence is not an issue here, and that the equilibrium is unique.

Now let us introduce tatonnement. Let r measure time in the tatonnement process. Rounds are held at regular intervals Δr, at times r_i ($i = 1, 2, \ldots$). The price that is called in round i is P_{r_i}, and the revealed demand for riskfree securities is h_{j,r_i}; that for risky securities is z_{j,r_i}. Between rounds, the auctioneer adjusts the prices in proportion to the excess demand:

$$\Delta P_r = P_{r_i} - P_{r_{i-1}} = \left[\sum_{j=1}^{Q} z_{j,r_{i-1}} - z^0 \right] \Delta r.$$

Plug in the formula for individual demands (1.43) to obtain:

$$\Delta P_r = \left[\sum_{j=1}^{Q} \frac{1}{b_j} \Sigma^{-1} (\mu - P_{r_{i-1}}) - z^0 \right] \Delta r. \qquad [1.44]$$

To facilitate the analysis, let the interval between two tatonnement rounds become smaller and smaller: $\Delta r \to 0$. In the limit, we get continuous adjustment. Let dP/dr denote the vector of derivatives of the price path with respect to tatonnement time. Simple algebra (see exercises) reveals:

$$\frac{dP}{dr} + \left[\sum_{j=1}^{Q} \frac{1}{b_j} \right] \Sigma^{-1} P = K, \qquad [1.45]$$

where the vector of constants K equals:

$$K = \left[\sum_{j=1}^{Q} \frac{1}{b_j} \right] \Sigma^{-1} \mu - z^0.$$

This is a standard system of ordinary differential equations.

In the exercises, the reader is asked to verify the following:

1. The unique stationary point of the system is the equilibrium in (1.43).
2. The system is globally stable (i.e., solutions converge to the stationary point from anywhere in the price space).

These points provide an answer to the question we set out to tackle, namely, how can markets find the CAPM equilibrium? We proposed that markets adjust as in our tatonnement model, and confirmed that, if so, they would discover equilibrium from anywhere in the price space.

There are at least two aspects of our tatonnement adjustment process that can be criticized. First, no transactions take place until the process has converged. In most financial markets (including the experimental markets of Chapter 3), transactions take place continuously, whether the market is in or out of equilibrium. That is, realistic price adjustment is nontatonnement.

Consequently, we should ask how robust our findings are to intermediate trade. They are unaffected, because of our assumption of constant absolute risk aversion, which implies that the aggregate excess demand, and hence, the price adjustment is independent of investors' wealth (see (1.44)). In other words, no matter how much investors gain or lose in the off-equilibrium transactions, it does not influence their demand in subsequent rounds.

Another way to see this is to notice that the equilibrium prices do not depend on the distribution of initial endowments of risky securities, but only on the total supply, z^0 (see (1.43)).

A second potential criticism concerns the adjustment of the price of the riskfree security. It is implicitly assumed in the standard tatonnement process that the riskfree security does not adjust independently to its own excess demand. This is because the entire analysis is carried out in terms of relative prices: the prices of the risky securities are expressed in terms of that of the riskfree security, and these relative prices adjust only to excess demand in their own market (see (1.44)).

Walrasian equilibrium restricts only relative prices, and our equilibrium is Walrasian. Therefore, it is standard practice to normalize the prices in terms of the price of some numeraire (in our case: the riskfree security).[10] One then carries out tatonnement analysis, as if the normalization that is justified in equilibrium remains possible out of equilibrium. It may, but it does imply a special adjustment process, because it does not allow the price of the numeraire to change separately as a function of excess demand in its own market.

The simplest way to force the excess demand in the numeraire to affect the price discovery process is to subtract it from the adjustment equation for each relative price. In our case, (1.44) changes to:

$$\Delta P_r = \left[\sum_{j=1}^{Q} \frac{1}{b_j} \Sigma^{-1} (\mu - P_{r_{i-1}}) - z^0 - \left(\sum_{j=1}^{Q} h_{j, r_{i-1}} - h^0 \right) \hat{1} \right] \Delta r, \quad [1.46]$$

where $\hat{1}$ denotes a vector of ones, and h^0 is the aggregate supply of riskfree securities ($h^0 = \sum_{j=1}^{Q} h_j^0$). If the excess demand for the riskfree security is positive, its absolute price increases, and hence, the relative prices of the risky securities decrease. The opposite is true if the excess demand for the riskfree security is negative.

In the limit, the price adjustment process in (1.46) becomes a system of ordinary differential equations:

$$\frac{dP}{dr} + \left[\sum_{j=1}^{Q} \frac{1}{b_j} \right] \Sigma^{-1} P - \left([\sum_{j=1}^{Q} \frac{1}{b_j}] [\Sigma^{-1} \mu] - z^0 \right)^T P \hat{1}$$

$$+ \left[\sum_{j=1}^{Q} \frac{1}{b_j} \right] P^T \Sigma^{-1} P \hat{1} = K, \quad [1.47]$$

where the vector of constants K equals:

$$K = \left[\sum_{j=1}^{Q} \frac{1}{b_j} \right] \Sigma^{-1} \mu - z^0.$$

This is Abel's system of ordinary differential equations of the first kind.

The system in (1.47) has several interesting properties. We single out two of them, relevant for our analysis. Exercises allow the reader to verify these:

---

10. Incidentally, in a RE equilibrium, one cannot readily normalize prices because absolute prices may carry information that is lost in the normalization.

1. The system can have several stationary points; only one of them is the CAPM equilibrium in (1.43).
2. The system is not globally stable, and the CAPM equilibrium may or may not be locally stable. The latter means that even if prices start out close to the equilibrium, they may never reach it.

These conclusions are troubling. They demonstrate that price discovery in the CAPM environment may be problematic if the price in the market for the riskfree security adjusts separately to its own excess demand, rather than through the excess demand in the risky securities, as in standard tatonnement analysis.

The latter demonstrates that the issue of price discovery in financial markets deserves far more attention than it has received so far. This section provides a framework for thinking about price discovery by staying within the competitive paradigm, rather than moving into strategic issues, which would undoubtedly complicate things.

Exercises

1. Prove (1.5), which is an application of the envelope theorem.
2. Prove that $\gamma = \delta$ in (1.13). (δ is defined in (1.1).)
3. Prove (1.22).
4. Demonstrate that portfolio separation obtains for general risk-averse preferences (i.e., $d\tilde{u}(c)/dc > 0$, $d^2\tilde{u}(c)/dc^2 < 0$) when (1.23) holds.
5. Prove that (1.21) holds in projections of excess returns on individual securities onto that of the market portfolio when the latter minimizes variance of return for a given mean (excess return).
6. Derive (1.30) and (1.31). (*Hint:* If $\ln X$ is normally distributed with mean μ and variance σ^2, then X is lognormal with mean $e^{\mu + \frac{1}{2}\sigma^2}$ and variance $e^{2\mu + \sigma^2}(e^{\sigma^2} - 1)$.)
7. Derive the Bellman function for a standard portfolio problem using the nonseparable utility function in (1.37), write down the first-order conditions, and use the envelope condition to prove (*).
8. Show that (1.26) and (1.43) are identical.

9. Prove that (1.45) has a unique stationary point, namely (1.43), and that the system is stable at this point.

10. Prove that (1.47) has multiple stationary points (how many exactly?), and evaluate stability at each point. Is (1.43) a stationary point, and, if so, is it always stable?

CHAPTER 2

Empirical Methodology

2.1 Introduction

The previous chapter gathered a few core predictions that theory makes about pricing in financial markets. Central is the hypothesis that markets equilibrate (although we did mention that this is not an obvious point), and that, in equilibrium, expected excess returns will be proportional to the covariance with aggregate risk (see (1.34)).

In bringing this theory to the data, there are several issues. The most important one concerns investors' beliefs. For the most part, we have assumed that beliefs were homogeneous (i.e., the same across investors), leaving open the possibility that these beliefs were wrong.

Intuitively, we should mean by "wrong" beliefs that they are not confirmed by the actual outcomes. There may be several reasons for this discrepancy between belief and reality. It may be that investors happened to hold more optimistic or pessimistic beliefs than was warranted. But it may also be that the empiricist was unable to collect an unbiased sample of outcomes, making it look as if the market held wrong beliefs, whereas the problem is really one of selection bias.

During virtually the entire theoretical development in the previous chapter, we did not have to assume that investors' beliefs were correct.

In other words, the theory allows there to be biases. When bringing the theory to bear on historical financial data, we then should allow for the possibility that investors' beliefs were biased at times. Otherwise, we are not providing a clean test of the theory. The test may fail because prices have historically been driven more by investors' mistaken expectations and their attempt to learn from their errors, and not because the theory is wrong per se.

That the theory is silent about investors' expectations poses a serious problem, however, because it means that the empiricist must estimate investors' beliefs as an integral component of a test of the theory.

The analysis of equilibrium existence in the previous chapter may have conveyed a different picture. We pointed out that conjectures about beliefs must be part of this analysis. The route that theorists chose was the most convenient one, namely, to assume a form of rationality restriction on beliefs called rational expectations (RE): investors correctly posit how prices relate to states. It is important to understand, however, that RE per se does not provide much of a restriction on beliefs, because it still allows investors to have arbitrary beliefs about the probability of occurrence of each state. (Although, as we mentioned, the two should be related, even if at present we do not know how.)

There is one major exception, namely, Lucas (1978). Lucas proved existence of an equilibrium where the mapping from states to prices is time-invariant. He considered the case where all state variables are stationary. To obtain the proof, Lucas had to make the bold assumption that investors' beliefs were correct (coincided with the true probability measure that governed the drawing of states). Otherwise, he would have had to include investors' beliefs as a state variable. If investors were aware that they had to learn, and this learning was convergent, then the belief state variable could not have been stationary, contrary to his assumption that all state variables were stationary.

Obviously, Lucas' assumption of correct beliefs is not needed if one does not insist on stationarity. See, for example, Radner (1972), where only RE is assumed. But stationarity does facilitate empirical analysis. This point will be one of the major themes of this chapter.

Finance academics have relied almost exclusively on the assumption of correct beliefs in the empirical analysis of historical data. The motivation for this is not based on theory (unlike Lucas), but merely on convenience. If one assumes that investors' beliefs are unbiased, then one can readily estimate expectations from empirical frequencies, provided a law of large numbers holds. In particular, expected returns and covariances of the general asset-pricing model in (1.34) can be estimated from historical average returns and sample covariances.

To estimate beliefs from empirical frequencies, a law of large numbers is needed. This readily obtains if the data (i.e., returns and consumption) are stationary, that is, are generated from a time-invariant distribution. The ergodic theorem then implies that empirical frequencies will converge to true frequencies, with which market beliefs are assumed to coincide.

The assumption that beliefs are correct and can be estimated from empirical frequencies (i.e., that returns and consumption are stationary) is known in the finance literature as the *efficient markets hypothesis* (EMH). This is not the usual definition that we can find in, say, Fama (1970), but as we will discuss, the usual definition is too vague. Because we state it in terms of unbiased beliefs and stationarity, our definition is clearer, and reflects the assumptions that underlie de facto inference in empirical research. That is, our definition focuses on what is actually being tested in empirical analysis.

The requirement that the data be stationary may at first be surprising. Stationarity is not always needed, however, as for instance in event studies. It is interesting to discover that event studies paint a more favorable picture of asset-pricing theory. (This says something about the validity of the stationarity assumption!) But let us not jump ahead. The empirical record will be discussed in Chapter 3.

Similar comments can be made about the first requirement for EMH, namely, that market beliefs are unbiased. The methodology exists to relax even this requirement. But we first have to produce evidence that we need to relax the assumption of unbiased beliefs. Much of the book argues that this assumption is indeed untenable in view of the data (and in support of the behavioral-finance critics). But we go beyond this. We show that attempts to allow for biases in beliefs go a long way toward explaining alleged asset-pricing anomalies.

EMH has its formal roots in Lucas's model, but was formulated much earlier (see, e.g., Fama [1970]). Lucas's model makes both assumptions: correctness of beliefs and stationarity. Lucas really proved that these assumptions are (or can be) mutually consistent. His model provides a framework for understanding some of the extreme claims of EMH. For instance, under EMH, average price changes (i.e., returns) reflect only risk (in addition to the time value of money), yet each price change reflects "news." Lucas's model explains how to reconcile these two statements.

EMH provides a link between statistics one can compute from historical data and the expectations and covariances of our asset-pricing theory. Once we establish this link, we continue the chapter with tests of the theory itself. We first explain how to test the CAPM, the consumption-based model, and Rubinstein's model. We end the chapter with a discussion of Hansen and Jagannathan's variance bounds, which provide a convenient way to illustrate one of the ways in which standard asset-pricing theory, together with EMH, has failed.

2.2   The Efficient Markets Hypothesis (EMH)

At the core of asset-pricing theory is the prediction that expected returns in excess of the riskfree rate should be proportional to the covariance with aggregate risk (see (1.34)).

In theory, the beliefs with which expectations and covariances are computed need not coincide with averages and covariances that one can estimate from subsequent realizations, even if the samples are large. That is, beliefs need not be unbiased. Hence, we ought to distinguish between investors' beliefs, on the one hand, and the probabilities that outcomes will subsequently factually be drawn. The simplest way would be to introduce a superscript m to expectations and covariances, where we refer to the "subjective" beliefs in the marketplace. When no such superscript is present, expectations and covariances are computed with respect to the "objective" probabilities. Let us do so, and rewrite the basic asset-pricing model, (1.34), as follows:

$$E^m[R_n|x] - R_F = -\text{cov}^m\left(\frac{A}{E[A|x]}, R_n|x\right).$$ [2.1]

EMH is the main building block of empirical asset-pricing theory. It is usually stated as *securities prices correctly reflect all available information.*

This is not a clear definition, because no yardstick is given about what "correctly" means. Most discussions regarding EMH have focused on what information can be reflected in prices (see, e.g., Grossman and Stiglitz [1980]), as opposed to what "correctly" signifies. One studies, for instance, how transactions can reveal private information. Although this is certainly an interesting question, asymmetric information has not yet been the concern of empirical asset-pricing studies, and hence, the issue need not occupy us here.

From a comprehensive reading of the empirical asset-pricing literature, one can distill the following two components to EMH. These do not constitute the usual definition, but reflect what is actually being assumed in the tests. They give content to the qualifier "correctly" in the usual definition. EMH assumes that:

1. Market beliefs are correct: ex ante expectations coincide with true expectations, and ex ante covariances correspond to true covariances.
2. Return distributions are time-invariant (i.e., stationary).

Under part 1 of this definition, (2.1) can be interpreted as:

$$E[R_n|x] - R_F = -\text{cov}\left(\frac{A}{E[A|x]}, R_n|x\right). \qquad [2.2]$$

Note that expectations and covariances are computed with the objective probability measure.

Part 2 of this definition may be surprising, but it has invariably been assumed in the empirical literature that objective expectations and covariances can be estimated by sample averages and covariances, which somehow must suppose stationarity. Indeed, stationarity implies that the law of large numbers holds (the ergodic theorem), so that sample moments estimate population or "objective" moments, provided the latter exist.[11]

---

11. The ergodic theorem states that if a stochastic process X_t, $t = 1, 2, \ldots$ has a time-invariant distribution (i.e., is stationary), then:

$$\lim_{T \to \infty} \frac{1}{T} \sum_{t=1}^{T} f(X_t) = E[f(X_1)], \text{ almost surely,}$$

provided $E[f(X_1)]$ exists.

As a matter of fact, the *tests* used to verify asset-pricing theory, such as the GMM test (see Hansen and Singleton [1982]), make even stronger assumptions, namely, that the data exhibit the right "mixing" conditions (i.e., their memory cannot be too long), so that central limit theorems obtain. The issues are very technical, and hence, we shy away from them. Some of the issues are addressed in Benink and Bossaerts (2001). We discuss the GMM test later in this chapter.

It is useful to explore some of the implications of our definition of EMH. In a static setting (to be understood as the case where the state vector does not enter the distribution of returns and aggregate risk), its main implication is that historical excess returns cannot be predicted beyond compensation for risk. Indeed, when applying EMH to (2.1), we not only are allowed to replace subjective expectations and covariances with objective quantities, but also with large-sample estimates of these quantities. Letting $\sim$ denote an equality that obtains asymptotically (i.e., as the sample size increases) and re-introducing t to index time, the prediction becomes, in the static case:

$$\frac{1}{T}\sum_{t=1}^{T}R_{n,t} - R_{F,t} \sim -\left(\frac{1}{T}\sum_{t=1}^{T}R_{n,t}\frac{A_t}{\left[\frac{1}{T}\sum_{t=1}^{T}A_t\right]} \right.$$
$$\left. -\left[\frac{1}{T}\sum_{t=1}^{T}R_{n,t}\right]\left[\frac{1}{T}\sum_{t=1}^{T}\frac{A_t}{\left[\frac{1}{T}\sum_{t=1}^{T}A_t\right]}\right] \right). \quad [2.3]$$

That is, historical average excess returns are proportional to historical covariances with aggregate risk.

The empirical statement in (2.3) leads to well-known corollaries. For instance, higher expected dividend growth will not show up in higher average excess returns, because, again, the statement simply says that average excess returns will reflect only risk.

One can turn this statement around: if an asset records extraordinarily high average excess returns (e.g., the U.S. stock markets in the 1990s), then it must be an exceptionally risky investment. One immediately sees that this leads to puzzles (what was the exceptional risk in the U.S. stock market in the 1990s?).

The dynamic versions of (2.1), that is, those cases where the conditioning on the state vector is nontrivial, are a bit more complex, because one cannot readily ignore conditioning information in the computation of covariances. Jensen's inequality causes a discrepancy between the expected covariance conditional on more information, on the one hand, and the covariance conditional on less information, on the other hand. We investigate this important complication in more depth later on. Suffice it to say that the claim that average excess returns cannot be predicted beyond compensation for risk remains valid in a dynamic context; but the compensation for risk no longer corresponds to the unconditional covariance with aggregate risk.

New students of asset pricing often find it paradoxical that average excess returns are determined only by risk, because the literature abounds with statements that prices must react to new information. Students may conclude that sample average excess returns must reflect the common message (e.g., optimistic, pessimistic) in the information flow over the sampling period being considered. Yet combined with EMH, the theory predicts that information somehow gets canceled out, and that average excess returns therefore reflect only risk.

This is best understood by reference to Lucas's RE model, which, as mentioned in the previous section, provides a theoretical framework for understanding the empirical asset-pricing literature. In Lucas's RE model, prices indeed react to information. Prices are a function of the state of the world: $P_n = \phi_n(x)$ (see the section 1.12 in Chapter 1). But average excess returns are still determined as in the definition of EMH above. Information is canceled out over the long run, leaving no room for information to affect average excess returns.

The stationarity of Lucas's world is the cause for this paradoxical situation. Stationarity implies that events repeat themselves. Lucas's assumption that investors' beliefs coincide with the objective probability measure implies that investors know this. This means that investors are never really surprised: they know all types of information that will ever emerge; they know that each type of information will occur repeatedly; and they know precisely the frequency with which this will happen. They almost have perfect foresight, except that they do not know exactly *when* a particular type of information is generated.[12]

---

12. This is like forecasting the weather. One knows that it rains with a certain frequency, but does not know when it will rain. It is not surprising that it rains on a given day.

In fact, because there are really no surprises in Lucas's world (and hence, in the world of EMH); one wonders why prices move at all. Basically, they move because bad information means that investors will temporarily have to be content with lower dividends. In the long run, nothing changes. These temporary dips in the dividend flow do reduce the price, if only marginally. An analogous situation holds for good news.

For reasonable parameter configurations, Lucas's model indeed predicts little volatility. Contrast this with the actual volatility of securities prices in the real world, and one has a puzzle. This is part of the *equity premium puzzle* of Mehra and Prescott (1985) that we discuss in depth later.

Since the stationarity assumption is so crucial to Lucas' model, and hence, to EMH, it is worth exploring how violations affect empirical findings. Let us do so now.

2.3   Violations of the Stationarity Assumption

To appreciate the importance of the stationarity assumption in EMH, let us study an example where stationarity is violated, while the other part of EMH—that beliefs are correct—still holds.

Of course, if beliefs are not correct, and investors know this, stationarity will automatically be violated (provided investors' learning improves the precision of their beliefs), as we pointed out earlier. Lucas introduced the assumption of correct beliefs to be consistent with his assumption that the state vector is stationary. Here, we ask the opposite: what happens if beliefs are correct but the world is nonstationary?

Nonstationarity is not necessarily a feature of the real world underlying the economy. It could be generated merely by the design of the securities traded. The most important example is equity, a claim on the assets of a firm whose value, if the firm is declared bankrupt, becomes zero and remains zero forever. (At least, that is how theory perceives the payoff on equity; actual bankruptcy laws may still assign value to equity even if a company declares bankruptcy.) Bankruptcy is a nonrepetitive event: it can happen only once. Hence, viewed as a stochastic process,

---

This is bound to happen with a known frequency. But it is surprising that it rains one day rather than another.

the return on equity cannot be stationary. Once a return of -100% is drawn, future returns are no longer well-defined, and one can claim that no value that occurred prior to bankruptcy will ever repeat.

Equity has been the focus of attention in research on the EMH, yet it violates one of the two main components of its definition, by design. Consequently, if inference is very much affected by the violation of stationarity, what is there to be learned from forty years of empirical research on equity prices?

We need an asset-pricing model, preferably a dynamic one, to investigate these issues. Because of its simplicity, Rubinstein's model is ideal. One could have chosen the CAPM, because of its status in empirical research, but this model is essentially static, and it takes quite some effort to generate it as a dynamic model (but see Stapleton and Subrahmanyam [1978], Chamberlain [1988] and Bossaerts and Green [1989]). We studied Rubinstein's model in Chapter 1, Section 7.

Rubinstein's model predicts the following for the relationship between the return on an asset n (R_n) and the return on the market portfolio (R_M):

$$E\left[\frac{1}{R_M}R_n|x\right] = 1.$$

(See (1.29).) We assume that investors hold correct beliefs. Consequently, we do not have to distinguish between subjective and objective probability measures in the computation of the above expectation.

Because nonstationarities will be present, however, we must reintroduce a time index. We continue to assume that the return on the market portfolio is stationary, so that the basic results that led to the above restriction remain valid (in particular, investors' consumption remains a fixed fraction of their wealth).

We are going to look at the world as a repetition (rounds) of the following two-period scenario. At the beginning of the first period, equity in a number of firms is available. Some of these firms survived from the previous round (i.e., they did not go bankrupt at the end of the previous round); others are newly created firms. At the end of the first period (coinciding with the beginning of the second period), news is released about the potential value of the firm at the end of the second period, including its chances to become bankrupt. This news remains noisy (i.e., investors will never be certain that a given firm will eventually go bankrupt). No dividend is paid. At the end of the second period, the status of the firm (bankrupt/not bankrupt) is announced. Equity in firms that declare bankruptcy pays zero dollars and disappears from the market subsequently; equity in firms that are not bankrupt continues to be traded in subsequent rounds; its end-of-second-period value equals its dividends plus the beginning-of-first-period market clearing price in the subsequent two-period round.

This image of the world as a concatenation of two-period rounds allows us to determine what the effects are of two distinct phenomena on inference about EMH, namely, (1) news about potential future bankruptcy, (2) bankruptcy announcements. It will become clear that inference is biased even if no bankruptcy occurs, but only news about its future likelihood is released (case (1)).

To clarify, let us refer to the first period as "January," and the second period as "the rest of the year." The time index t will be used to refer to rounds of two periods, and J denotes January, and O denotes the rest of the year. Rubinstein's model predicts that, over January:

$$E\left[\frac{1}{R_{M,t,J}} R_{n,t,J} | x_{t,J}\right] = 1, \qquad [2.4]$$

and, over the rest of the year:

$$E\left[\frac{1}{R_{M,t,O}} R_{n,t,O} | x_{t,O}\right] = 1. \qquad [2.5]$$

$x_{t,J}$ denotes the state vector at the beginning of January; it includes all the information that investors need to determine the distribution of the subsequent returns. $x_{t,O}$ denotes the state vector at the beginning of the rest of the year.

We can rewrite (2.4) and (2.5) in terms of expected excess returns and covariances with risk, as in (2.2), namely,

$$E[R_{n,t,J} - R_{F,t,J} | x_{t,J}] = -\text{cov}\left(\frac{R_{F,t,J}}{R_{M,t,J}}, R_{n,t,J} | x_{t,J}\right), \qquad [2.6]$$

$$E[R_{n,t,O} - R_{F,t,O} | x_{t,O}] = -\text{cov}\left(\frac{R_{F,t,O}}{R_{M,t,O}}, R_{n,t,O} | x_{t,O}\right). \qquad [2.7]$$

These are the assumptions on the distribution of the return on the market. To simplify, we employ two-point (binomial) distributions. Although the results do not depend on them, we use specific numerical values. In the beginning of January, the market starts out with a value of one dollar. At the end of January, its value equals $s_{M,t}$, which is either 0.9 or 1.2. At the end of the year, its value equals the product of $s_{M,t}$ and another random variable, $\theta_{M,t}$, which also is either 0.9 or 1.2. The joint distribution of $s_{M,t}$ and $\theta_{M,t}$ is:

$$P(\theta_{M,t} = 0.9, s_{M,t} = 0.9) = 0.3$$

$$P(\theta_{M,t} = 0.9, s_{M,t} = 1.2) = 0.1$$

$$P(\theta_{M,t} = 1.2, s_{M,t} = 0.9) = 0.2$$

$$P(\theta_{M,t} = 1.2, s_{M,t} = 1.2) = 0.4.$$

By applying Bayes's law, one can easily infer the conditional probabilities of $\theta_{M,t}$, given $s_{M,t}$, which are needed for investors to determine the distribution of the market return at the beginning of the rest of the year.

We consider the pricing of a share of equity in firm n, whose payoff at the end of the year equals the *product* of four binomial random variables, $s_{n,t}$, $\theta_{n,t}$, and the square of the two random variables that determine the payoff on the market portfolio, that is, $(s_{M,t})^2$ and $(\theta_{M,t})^2$.[13] Thus the end-of-year payoff on equity in firm n equals:

$$s_{n,t}\theta_{n,t}(s_{M,t})^2(\theta_{M,t})^2.$$

Like $s_{M,t}$, $s_{n,t}$ is revealed at the end of January; $\theta_{n,t}$ and $\theta_{M,t}$ are revealed at the end of the year. We will assume that the distribution of $s_{n,t}$ and $\theta_{n,t}$ is independent of that of $s_{M,t}$ and $\theta_{M,t}$. By letting the payoff on the equity in firm n depend on $\theta_{M,t}$, we generate a correlation between the return on the equity in firm n and the market portfolio.

The variable $s_{n,t}$ takes on the values 1 and 2, whereas $\theta_{n,t}$ can be either 0 or 1. When $\theta_{n,t}$ equals 0, the equity's value at the end of the year is zero, and hence, the firm is bankrupt. We will assume that $s_{n,t}$ and $\theta_{n,t}$ are correlated with each other, so that $s_{n,t}$ signals information about the likelihood of bankruptcy at the end of the year. In particular, let us take the following numerical values:

13. We take the square of the binomial random variables that determine the market payoff, because otherwise, the risk premium on firm n would equal that of the market, given the independence assumptions we state later on. In an exercise, the reader is asked to verify this claim.

$$P(\theta_{n,t} = 0, s_{n,t} = 1) = 0.05$$

$$P(\theta_{n,t} = 0, s_{n,t} = 2) = 0.02$$

$$P(\theta_{n,t} = 1, s_{n,t} = 1) = 0.35$$

$$P(\theta_{n,t} = 1, s_{n,t} = 2) = 0.58.$$

Hence, the firm declares bankruptcy with probability 0.07. Bayes's law allows the investors to compute conditional probabilities. For instance, the conditional probability of bankruptcy in the event $s_{n,t} = 1$ is $0.05/(0.05 + 0.35)$, or $1/8$.

Because we assume that $s_{n,t}$ and $\theta_{n,t}$ are independent of $s_{M,t}$ and $\theta_{M,t}$, bankruptcy, as well as news about bankruptcy, are idiosyncratic, that is, are unrelated to the return on the market portfolio. Another way to state this is that bankruptcy risk can be diversified away by buying the market portfolio.

Tedious algebra (details are in the Exercises) reveals the following. First, the riskfree rate is 2.9% in January, 0% over the rest of the year if $s_{M,t} = 0.9$, and 12.5% otherwise. The expected return on the market is 5.0% in January and 2.0% over the rest of the year if $s_M = 0.9$, and 14.0% otherwise. These are expected returns; we comment shortly on whether they can be estimated in an unbiased way from historical averages.

Likewise, one can verify that the expected January return on equity of firm n equals 8.0%, whereas that over the rest of the year equals 4.1% if $s_{M,t} = 0.9$, and 15.3% otherwise. Again, these are expected returns and may deviate from what one could infer on average in historical records.

What can we learn from historical averages? Let us first consider the case where an empiricist collects January returns over T years (rounds), $t = 1, \ldots, T$, and suppose that firm n did not declare bankruptcy during this time. That is, $\theta_{n,t} = 1, t = 1, \ldots, T$. Notice that bankruptcy is never declared in January, so, if we find biases in the inference, it can only be caused by news about bankruptcy.

First, consider the sample average excess return on the market portfolio:

$$\frac{1}{T} \sum_{t=1}^{T} (R_{M,t,J} - R_{F,t,J}).$$

In expectation, and conditional on firm n not defaulting, this sample average equals:

$$E\left[\frac{1}{T}\sum_{t=1}^{T}(R_{M,t,J} - R_{F,t,J})|\theta_{n,t} = 1, \ t = 1, \dots, T\right]$$

$$= E\left[\frac{1}{T}\sum_{t=1}^{T}(R_{M,t,J} - R_{F,t,J})\right]$$

$$= 2.1\%, \qquad\qquad\qquad [2.8]$$

because bankruptcy risk is idiosyncratic. Consequently, the empiricist has an unbiased estimate of the market risk premium.

Now look at the sample average excess return on the equity of firm n:

$$\frac{1}{T}\sum_{t=1}^{T}(R_{n,t,J} - R_{F,t,J}).$$

Bayes's law allows us to compute the expectation of this sample average, conditional on firm n not defaulting. This reveals:

$$E\left[\frac{1}{T}\sum_{t=1}^{T}(R_{n,t,J} - R_{F,t,J})|\theta_{n,t} = 1, \ t = 1, \dots, T\right] = 6.8\%, \quad [2.9]$$

which is significantly higher than the expected excess return of 5.1% (= 8.0%–2.9%). The empiricist does not compare this number with the true risk premium (i.e., the left hand side of (2.6)), but with its sample version, computed from a history when the firm did not declare bankruptcy. The sample estimate of the risk premium is denoted by ρ_T:

$$\rho_T = -\frac{1}{T}\sum_{t=1}^{T}\left(\frac{R_{F,t,J}}{R_{M,t,J}}R_{n,t,J}\right) + \left(\frac{1}{T}\sum_{t=1}^{T}\frac{R_{F,t,J}}{R_{M,t,J}}\right)\left(\frac{1}{T}\sum_{t=1}^{T}R_{n,t,J}\right).$$

Conditional on $\theta_{n,t} = 1, t = 1, \dots, T$, the expected value of this sample estimate equals:

$$E[\rho_T|\theta_{n,t} = 1, \ t = 1, \dots, T] = 5.2\%, \qquad [2.10]$$

which is comparable to the ex ante risk premium of 5.1%.

Notice two points: (1) the estimated risk premium is close to the actual risk premium (5.2% vs. 5.1%); (2) the expected sample average excess return is much higher, namely, 6.8%. Comparing the two, we conclude that *the empiricist is likely to reject Rubinstein's model, incorrectly.* More precisely, the empiricist would find *overperformance for equity of firms that could have declared default but happen not to have done so.*

Because small firms have historically had a higher probability to declare bankruptcy, it is natural to ask whether the above explains why their equity has been experiencing abnormally large excess returns (see, e.g., Fama and French [1992]; but see Cochrane [1999] for cautionary notes, because this "size effect" has apparently disappeared recently).

The above illustrates the main point of this section: it is possible to reject an asset-pricing model (like Rubinstein's), not because it is wrong, but because there are nonstationarities (or nonrepetitive events) in the data, caused by, in this case, bankruptcy.

Analogous conclusions hold for sample average excess returns and estimated risk premiums over the rest of the year. As in January, the market's ex ante expected return can be estimated in an unbiased way. In contrast, the sample average excess return on the equity in a firm that did not declare bankruptcy is biased upward. In expectation, it equals 11.7%, whereas the ex ante expected excess return equals 3.4%. The ex post measured risk premium is still close to the ex ante value: 3.7%.[14] Consequently, equity in firm n generates historical excess returns well above its estimated risk premium, leading one to conclude falsely that Rubinstein's model is wrong.

It is no use to add firms that did default in the history being analyzed. There is an exception, namely, if such firms always declare bankruptcy in year T, where T equals one over the ex ante probability of bankruptcy— $1/0.07$ in the numerical example. Of course, this is unlikely.

What causes the biased inference? Consider what happens in a single year t. Ex ante, both $\theta_{n,t} = 0$ (default) and $\theta_{n,t} = 1$ (survival) are possible. Ex post, however, only one will occur, and, if $\theta_{n,t} = 0$, the firm defaults,

14. These numbers are expectations across all possible states at the end of January. The following table lists the possible states (values of $s_{n,t}$ and $s_{M,t}$), their unconditional (ex ante) and conditional (on $\theta_{n,t} = 1$, $t = 1, \ldots, T$) probabilities ("prob" and "cond prob," respectively), their unconditional and conditional expected *excess* returns ("ex ante xret" and "ex post xret," respectively), and their conditional expected estimated risk premium ("ex post rp"). The column "all" displays the expectations across all states.

$(s_{n,t}, s_{M,t})$	(1,0.9)	(1,1.2)	(2,0.9)	(2,1.2)	all
prob	0.20	0.20	0.30	0.30	1
cond prob	0.19	0.19	0.31	0.31	1
ex ante xret (%)	4.1	2.8	4.1	2.8	3.4
ex post xret (%)	19.0	19.2	7.8	6.7	11.7
ex post rp (%)	4.7	3.2	4.3	2.9	3.7

and will disappear. Default is a nonrecurring event, and hence, the time series of returns on equity will not be stationary; nonstationarity causes the bias.

2.4   Inference in a Nonstationary World

It is possible to avoid the stationarity assumption by investigating the *cross-sectional* patterns of excess returns rather than the time series of a single equity issue. In a given year t, the average number of bankruptcy declarations equals the ex ante expected number on average, according to EMH (i.e., ex ante beliefs are correct). Let there be N identical firms, and compute the cross-sectional average excess return in January:

$$\frac{1}{N} \sum_{n=1}^{N} R_{n,t,J} - R_{F,t,J}.$$

That over the rest of the year equals:

$$\frac{1}{N} \sum_{n=1}^{N} R_{n,t,O} - R_{F,t,O}.$$

The expected values of these statistics are simply the ex ante expected excess return on equity of any single firm:

$$E\left[\frac{1}{N} \sum_{n=1}^{N} R_{n,t,J} - R_{F,t,J} \right] = E\left[R_{n,t,J} - R_{F,t,J} \right]$$

and:

$$E\left[\frac{1}{N} \sum_{n=1}^{N} R_{n,t,O} - R_{F,t,O} \right] = E\left[R_{n,t,O} - R_{F,t,O} \right].$$

Although the ex ante expected excess returns can be estimated in an unbiased way from the cross-sectional average historical excess return in a given year, it is not obvious how to obtain good estimates of the required risk premium (i.e., the covariance term on the right hand side of (2.6) and (2.7)), because the return on the market portfolio is constant in cross-section.

One can still obtain a good estimate of the required risk premium, however, by sampling different firms over different years: the return on the equity in firm n is taken from year t_n (the subscript n reflects the fact that t changes with n) and matched with the return on the market in the same year. For instance, the January risk premium is estimated as follows:

$$-\frac{1}{N}\sum_{n=1}^{N}\left(\frac{R_{F,t_n J}}{R_{M,t_n J}}R_{n,t_n J}\right) + \left(\frac{1}{N}\sum_{n=1}^{N}\frac{R_{F,t_n J}}{R_{M,t_n J}}\right)\left(\frac{1}{N}\sum_{t=n}^{N}R_{n,t_n J}\right). \quad [2.11]$$

This risk premium is then to be compared to the historical average excess January return estimated in an analogous way:

$$\frac{1}{N}\sum_{n=1}^{N}R_{n,t_n J} - R_{F,t_n J}. \quad [2.12]$$

The attentive reader will have suspected that (2.12) is a standard estimate for the expected excess return in *event studies*. In that context, (t_n, J) and (t_n, O) are usually certain time periods after a well-determined event, such as an earnings announcement, or an initial public offering (IPO). For example, (t_n, J) may be the first period (month, half-year, . . .) after the IPO of firm n, and (t_n, O) may refer to the period thereafter. Of course, the risk premium will be estimated with precision only if the events are not clustered in (calendar) time, for otherwise the return on the market portfolio may not vary sufficiently across observations.

In event studies, the risk premium has generally not been estimated as in (2.11). Often, the CAPM is assumed, as opposed to Rubinstein's model (which forms the basis for (2.11)). Sometimes estimation of the risk premium is avoided entirely by comparing the excess return around the time of an event to that of event-free firms that are carefully matched in terms of risk.

What the foregoing demonstrates is that event studies provide a way to test asset-pricing theory on only one part of the EMH assumption, namely, that investors' ex ante beliefs are correct. Stationarity is not needed, which means that event study methodology is particularly appropriate to investigating the pricing of equity.

Consequently, it is not surprising that the support of asset-pricing theory from event studies has generally been more favorable than the impressions one gathers from tests based on time series analysis. We come back to this point in Chapter 3, which discusses the empirical evidence.

Some readers may not associate event studies with tests of asset-pricing theory. The average price reaction (or sign) around an event, they may claim, is the focus of attention, and not any asset-pricing theory. Still, one cannot always evaluate the meaning of the average price reaction without reference to asset-pricing theory. For instance, one may misinterpret a significantly positive average excess return on an event day as a reaction to the news that is being released, as opposed to the realization of a risk premium. This confusion certainly occurs when the event itself (e.g., earnings announcements) is predictable. In that case, any evaluation of how the market reacted to the news must filter out risk premium effects, and so, must be based on asset-pricing theory. [15]

In addition, event studies often analyze stock performance for a period after an event. One cannot evaluate whether the after-event returns are rational without reference to asset-pricing theory, because risk is present; thus our remarks become relevant.

For completeness, it should be added that the CAPM can be tested on a cross-section of asset returns even if these are clustered in time. This is specific to the CAPM, and requires a particular testing strategy. The analysis is rather technical, and so not included here. The interested reader is referred to Bossaerts and Hillion (1995).

2.5   Testing the CAPM

Let us return to EMH and assume stationarity. Also, let us return to the asset-pricing model that has been most popular in empirical analysis of historical data, namely, the CAPM. The main prediction of the CAPM is that the market portfolio of risky securities will be mean-variance optimal. This implies (1.26), namely,

$$E[R_n - R_F|x] = \beta_{n,x}^M E[R_M - R_F|x].$$

15. The event study in Chari, Jagannathan, and Offer (1988) is a case in point. They find that equity prices increase on average on earnings announcements, independent of whether the earnings news was positive (higher earnings than expected) or negative (lower earnings than expected). They interpret this as the realization of a risk premium. This interpretation is presumably correct, but one cannot be sure of it without computing the required risk premium, that is, without computing the covariance in (2.2).

The risk measure, $\beta_{n,x}^M$, is the slope in a linear projection of the excess return on security n onto that of the market portfolio.

The projection on which the risk measure is based, as well as the expectations it constrains, are *conditional* on the state vector x, which represents all the information that the investors use to determine their trades, and hence, prices. In most of the empirical literature, conditioning has been ignored. Later we question whether this is justified, other than in a world where investment opportunities are independent and identical replications from one period to another.

In the meanwhile, let us drop the conditioning to simplify the notation. In other words, we are interested in a test of the following:

$$E[R_n - R_F] = \beta_n^M E[R_M - R_F]. \qquad [2.13]$$

There are several ways to test (2.13), discussed below.

2.5.1 A Linear Test

The most obvious test is based on ordinary least squares (OLS) estimation of the intercept and slope in:

$$R_n - R_F = \alpha_n^M + \beta_n^M (R_M - R_F) + \epsilon_n^M$$

(see also (1.24)), and to test the null that:

$$\boxed{\alpha_n^M = 0,} \qquad \text{for all } n.$$

The test is a simple linear test of a number of intercepts. Under the assumption of normality, the small-sample properties of this test can be derived explicitly. See Gibbons, Ross, and Shanken (1989), who also demonstrate that the above test is identical to testing whether the Sharpe ratio (average excess return divided by standard deviation) of the market portfolio is maximal, which would be a direct test of CAPM's prediction that the market portfolio is mean-variance optimal.

The intercept in the above projection has become known as *Jensen's alpha*. It features prominently not only in tests of the CAPM, but also in portfolio performance evaluation.

In principle, the CAPM holds only if $\alpha_n^M = 0$, for all n. Feasibility of the above test requires that the number of securities (N) be smaller than the length of the time series (T) over which the projections are executed. Unfortunately, N is usually large in comparison to any T over which empiricists are willing to assume stationarity. To restore feasibility, empiricists have long chosen to group securities in portfolios, based on prior-period beta, size, book-to-market ratio, and so on.

It is worth pointing out that such grouping into portfolios obviously reduces the power of the tests. It can be shown, for instance, that if the grouping generates well-diversified portfolios (which implicitly requires that returns exhibit a sort of weak factor structure), then the above test is empty provided there are no arbitrage opportunities. That is, the CAPM will never be rejected, even if it does not hold, unless there are arbitrage opportunities. See Bossaerts and Hillion (1995) for analysis and proof.

2.5.2   A Nonlinear Test

Rather than using excess returns, one could also use raw returns, thereby avoiding the assumption that a riskfree security exists, a case that we have not considered so far. The latter would imply that the ensuing test is more robust.

Practically, the slope and intercept are estimated in the following projection:

$$R_n = \alpha_n^M + \beta_n^M R_M + \epsilon_n^M.$$

We then test whether there exists a coefficient γ, common across securities, such that:

$$\boxed{\alpha_n^M = (1 - \beta_n^M)\gamma.}$$

This is a set of nonlinear tests, which means that distributional properties of the test statistics it generates will have to be based on large-sample theory (large T), substantially reducing its appeal (see, e.g., Gibbons [1982]).

As mentioned before, the nonlinear test is more robust, in principle. It does not require the existence of a riskfree security, and hence, one would expect that if the nonlinear test rejects, then the linear test must also reject, except if the riskfree rate that the empiricist uses is not perceived to be riskfree (in real terms) by investors.

It is then surprising that the nonlinear test generally rejects the CAPM, whereas it is much harder for the linear test to reject the CAPM. This unexpected result is discussed in Gibbons, Ross, and Shanken (1989) and Bossaerts and Green (1989). One could conjecture that the asymptotic arguments that are the basis of the nonlinear test are unreliable given typical values for T (usually, 60 observations of one-month returns). Another, perhaps more plausible explanation would be to point to the behavior of the riskfree rate: its autocorrelation is fairly high—near 1—to the point that it starts affecting inference. The coefficient γ somehow estimates the average riskfree rate. But the average of a highly autocorrelated time series is notoriously unstable (i.e., displays a high standard error), whereas the nonlinear test works best when it is fixed. By subtracting out the riskfree rate, the linear test avoids the problem of instability, and hence, leads to a cleaner test.

The empirical literature has not given much attention to this paradoxical situation. Further scrutiny does not seem inappropriate, given the controversial nature of the empirical evidence surrounding the CAPM (see Chapter 3).

2.5.3   The Fama-MacBeth Procedure

A very popular test of the CAPM is the following two-step procedure:

1. Use least squares (LS) to estimate β_n^M in the following time series projection:

$$R_n = \alpha_n^M + \beta_n^M R_M + \epsilon_n^M.$$

   Let $\hat{\beta}_n^M$ denote the LS estimate.

2. For each period, run the following *cross-sectional* projection (i.e., across n):

$$R_n = \gamma_0 + \gamma_1 \hat{\beta}_n^M + \eta_n. \qquad [2.14]$$

   Test whether, across periods, $\gamma_1 > 0$ on average. Also, does γ_0 equal the riskfree rate on average?

In this *Fama-MacBeth procedure*, based on Fama and MacBeth (1973), the time series average γ_1 is an estimate of the expected excess return on the market portfolio, and hence, must be positive for the CAPM to hold. Likewise, γ_0 must equal the riskfree rate, on average.

There is an errors-in-variables problem in the Fama-MacBeth procedure: the explanatory variable in the second step should be β_n^M, but the estimate $\hat{\beta}_n^M$ replaces it. Hence, there is an estimation error. To mitigate it, empiricists often use the beta of a portfolio for $\hat{\beta}_n^M$. The beta of a portfolio can be estimated with much more precision. Portfolios are associated with individual securities on the basis of some criterion such as size of the issue or book-to-market ratio of the firm issuing the security.

In fact, because such criteria as size and book-to-market ratio constitute prior information for investors, assigning portfolio betas to individual securities may be interpreted as a way to accommodate conditioning in the Fama-MacBeth procedure. In principle, betas have to be computed conditional on investors' information x (see (1.26)). So far, the CAPM tests that we have discussed do not condition on x. By assigning, say, the beta of the size-decile portfolio to which a security belongs before a given period, one effectively uses conditional betas. Therefore, the Fama-MacBeth procedure appears to provide a test of the CAPM that is closer to the theory of asset pricing.

The only potential problem is that the assignment is usually based on one or at most two criteria, such as size, or size and book-to-market ratio (see, e.g., Fama and French [1992]). Size and book-to-market ratio constitute only two elements of the entire information set of the state vector x that could be argued to be relevant for investors in determining trades, and hence, prices. One wonders whether the Fama-MacBeth procedure is robust to deleting the remaining information. That is, if investors' perception of a security's risk is based on a conditional beta $\beta_{x,n}^M$ that is computed from a richer state variable x than the empiricist is using, one may falsely reject the CAPM. (Technically, we should phrase this as "one may reject the CAPM more often than the nominal size of the test.")

Let us turn to this important question of whether empiricists can ignore relevant conditioning information without biasing their CAPM test.

2.5.4 Can One Condition on Less than the Entire State Vector in Tests of the CAPM?

Yes, one can condition on less than the entire state vector x, but not in the Fama-MacBeth procedure. Jensen's inequality explains why the Fama-MacBeth procedure is biased.

To see this, let us assume that betas are computed conditionally on a piece of the state vector x—say, the book-to-market ratios corresponding to all securities in the sample. Let x_b denote this subvector. To focus on the issue of conditioning, ignore the errors-in-variables problem (i.e., take the estimate of the conditional beta, $\hat{\beta}^M_{n,x_b}$, to be the true conditional beta, β^M_{n,x_b}). The empiricist runs the second-step regression as follows:

$$R_n = \gamma_0 + \gamma_1 \beta^M_{n,x_b} + \eta_n. \quad [2.15]$$

She tests whether γ_0 equals the riskfree rate on average, and whether the average γ_1 is strictly positive. The latter would be an estimate of the average excess return on the market portfolio, which has to be positive for the market to be mean-variance optimal.

Does the theory really make these predictions? The CAPM states that, in equilibrium:

$$E[R_n - R_F|x] = \beta^M_{n,x}E[R_M - R_F|x].$$

See (1.26). To compute the beta, however, the empiricist conditioned only on x_b, and not the entire state vector x. Does the restriction survive with β^M_{n,x_b} if we take expectations? (Technically, this is called "conditioning down to x_b.") In general, the answer is no. Take expectations and apply the law of iterated expectations as fully as possible:

$$E[R_n - R_F|x_b]$$
$$= E[E[R_n - R_F|x]|x_b]$$
$$= E[\beta^M_{n,x}E[R_M - R_F|x]|x_b]$$
$$= \text{cov}(\beta^M_{n,x}, E[R_M - R_F|x]|x_b) + E[\beta^M_{n,x}|x_b]E[E[R_M - R_F|x]|x_b]$$
$$= \text{cov}(\beta^M_{n,x}, E[R_M - R_F|x]|x_b) + E[\beta^M_{n,x}|x_b]E[R_M - R_F|x_b].$$

We clearly do not obtain what we wanted. Even if we were to argue that $\text{cov}(\beta^M_{n,x}, E[R_M - R_F|x]|x_b)$ equals zero, we still need $E[\beta^M_{n,x}|x_b] = \beta^M_{n,x_b}$, which generally does not obtain, because of Jensen's inequality. In other words, the CAPM does not imply that:

$$E[R_n - R_F|x_b] = \beta^M_{n,x_b}E[R_M - R_F|x_b],$$

which is what the empiricist tests with (2.15).

Consequently, although applications of the Fama-MacBeth procedure as in Fama and French (1992) seem to be interpretable as providing legitimate tests of the CAPM that account for the conditioning that is part of the theory, they are not, because only a subset of the available conditioning information is used.

Of course, one could object that it will never be manageable to condition on all the information that may have been relevant to investors. Thus, the question emerges whether there is a testing procedure that allows the empiricist to condition on a subset of investors' information.

There is, based on a simple application of the ideas developed in Hansen and Singleton (1982). We emphasized before that the CAPM makes one major prediction, namely, that the market portfolio is mean-variance optimal. Why not test this directly? Why not verify whether we can find a quadratic utility function such that a person with these preferences would find it optimal to hold the market portfolio? This can readily be done by finding the preference parameters such that the first-order conditions (stochastic Euler equations) are satisfied.

Recall the first-order conditions for quadratic preferences, (1.16): with an optimal portfolio, an investor with preference parameters δ, a, and b generates future wealth x'_1, such that, for some λ,

$$\delta E[(a - bx'_1)R_n|x] = \lambda,$$

for all n. Subtracting the first-order condition for the riskfree security, this implies:

$$E[(a - bx'_1)(R_n - R_F)|x] = 0, \qquad [2.16]$$

for all n. To test the CAPM, one verifies whether there are parameters a and b such that these conditions can be satisfied when x'_1 is the future value of the market portfolio. Thus one tests whether holding the market portfolio is ever optimal for quadratic preferences (i.e., whether the market portfolio is mean-variance optimal).

A test of the moment restrictions (2.16) need not involve the entire state vector x. The empiricist can condition on any subvector x_b: from the law of iterated expectations, (2.16) implies that:

$$E[E[(a - bx'_1)(R_n - R_F)|x]|x_b] = E[(a - bx'_1)(R_n - R_F)|x_b] = 0.$$

That is, the restrictions remain formally the same, even after conditioning down to x_b.

The ability to ignore relevant information is important, because it means that tests of the CAPM can be robust. The empiricist will never be able to state confidently that she has taken into account all information that could have been relevant for investors in determining their trading, and hence, prices. The Fama-MacBeth method (let alone the linear or nonlinear test that we discussed before the Fama-MacBeth method) is sensitive to conditioning information. A test based on (2.16) is not.

The restrictions in (2.16) generate a test only in principle. Implementation raises some tough statistical issues: although the excess return inside the expectation $(R_n - R_F)$ may be taken to be stationary, the end-of-period wealth, x'_1, may not, at least not if it is identified with the value of the market portfolio. Because of lack of stationarity, the expectation in (2.16) may not be estimated consistently. (Earlier in this chapter, we emphasized the importance of stationarity in the estimation of expectations.) To restore stationarity, scaling with the beginning-of-period wealth x_1 is necessary. It is not clear how to introduce plausibly the normalization. Perhaps one could let the preference parameter a depend on beginning-of-period wealth x_1 as well. But this seems to invalidate the logic that led to (2.16). In particular, the envelope condition could no longer be used to substitute the marginal utility of end-of-period wealth for the derivative of the Bellman function (see the discussion following (1.5)).

An alternative is to move away from the CAPM and go directly to a fully consistent dynamic asset-pricing model, such as Rubinstein's model. His model is directly cast in terms of stochastic Euler equations, and hence, tests are immediately robust to ignoring relevant information. Recall his model (see (1.29)):

$$E\left[\frac{1}{R_M}R_n|x\right] = 1,$$

for all n. This restriction continues to hold relative to a subvector x_b of x. Taking expectations conditional on x_b on both sides generates:

$$E\left[E\left[\frac{1}{R_M}R_n|x\right]|x_b\right] = E\left[\frac{1}{R_M}R_n|x_b\right] = 1.$$

In Rubinstein's model, no parameter must be estimated. Consequently, the model can be readily tested. The easiest way to do this is by the method of moments. One collects a time series of T returns on N securities and the market portfolio, and then tests whether the sample average:

$$\frac{1}{T}\sum_{t=1}^{T}\frac{1}{R_{M,t}}R_{n,t},$$

is significantly different from 1.

Such a method of moments test has become the basis for tests of consumption-based asset-pricing models. Let us turn to these models now.

2.6   Testing Consumption-Based Asset-Pricing Models

As for Rubinstein's model, the restrictions that consumption-based asset-pricing models impose on the data come directly out of a representative agent's first-order conditions for optimal investment and consumption, namely, (1.28), which is reproduced here for ease of reference:

$$\delta E\left[\frac{\frac{\partial \tilde{u}(c_A')}{\partial c'}}{\frac{\partial \tilde{u}(c_A)}{\partial c}}R_n\Big|x\right] = 1,$$

for all n. This model can be tested on time series of securities returns (R_n) and aggregate consumption (c_A). The utility function must, however, be parametrized.

One popular choice of preferences is power utility, that is,

$$\tilde{u}(c_A) = \frac{(c_A)^{\gamma+1}}{\gamma+1}. \qquad [2.17]$$

Risk aversion requires decreasing marginal utility of consumption, and hence, $\gamma < 0$. Substitution into the above stochastic Euler equations generates:

$$\delta E\left[\left(\frac{c_A'}{c_A}\right)^{\gamma}R_n\Big|x\right] = 1. \qquad [2.18]$$

Tests are based on the sample equivalent of the theoretical moment restrictions in (2.18). Notice that the theoretical moments can readily be estimated from time series, if there is no evidence against the hypothesis that both returns (R_n) and consumption growth (c_A'/c_A) are stationary. The ergodic theorem implies that sample moments estimate the theoretical moments in a consistent way.

The most straightforward test is based on the unconditional version of (2.18), namely,

$$\delta E\left[\left(\frac{c_A'}{c_A}\right)^{\gamma}R_n\right] = 1, \qquad [2.19]$$

for all n. These moment conditions can be tested by finding values for δ and γ to minimize the distance of the sample averages:

$$\delta \frac{1}{T} \sum_{t=1}^{T} \left(\frac{c_{A,t}}{c_{A,t-1}} \right)^{\gamma} R_{n,t}$$

(for all n) and 1, and checking whether the minimum distance is likely to obtain by chance. This is the GMM test first suggested in Hansen and Singleton (1982).

More sophisticated tests are based on elements in the state vector called instruments. (These also apply to Rubinstein's model.) Let x_b be one such instrument. The restriction in (2.18) continues to hold after multiplying the right and left hand side with x_b:

$$\delta E \left[\left(\frac{c_A'}{c_A} \right)^{\gamma} R_n x_b | x \right] = x_b.$$

Taking expectations:

$$\delta E \left[\left(\frac{c_A'}{c_A} \right)^{\gamma} R_n x_b \right] = E[x_b]. \qquad [2.20]$$

The latter can be tested by finding the values of δ and γ that minimize the distance between the sample averages

$$\delta \frac{1}{T} \sum_{t=1}^{T} \left(\frac{c_{A,t}}{c_{A,t-1}} \right)^{\gamma} R_{n,t} x_{b,t}$$

(for all n) and:

$$\frac{1}{T} \sum_{t=1}^{T} x_{b,t},$$

and checking whether the minimum distance is significantly different from zero.

See Hansen and Singleton (1982) and Epstein and Zin (1991) for examples.

There is clearly one weak spot in the GMM methodology, namely, the choice of instruments. A priori, anything that could even remotely be relevant information for investors (i.e., anything that could possibly be in the state vector x) is a potential instrument. But if an instrument is chosen that has no bearing on either future consumption or future returns, the moment conditions in (2.20) hold by construction once parameter values are chosen so that (2.19) holds. In this case:

$$\delta E\left[\left(\frac{c_A'}{c_A}\right)^\gamma R_n x_b\right] = \delta E\left[\left(\frac{c_A'}{c_A}\right)^\gamma R_n\right] E[x_b]$$
$$= 1 E[x_b]$$
$$= E[x_b].$$

Even if more than two securities are used, the GMM test may lack power. For instance, assume $N = 3$. This will generate six moment conditions: three versions of (2.19) and three versions of (2.20). There are two parameters to be estimated, namely, δ and γ. So, in principle, one has four degrees of freedom on which to reject the theory. But three of these are spurious, namely, the three versions of (2.20), because they are but replications of the three versions of (2.19). That leaves one with one degree of freedom. Yet the χ^2 test that is used in GMM will count four degrees of freedom, and hence, the test is unlikely to reject a false theory.

We discuss the evidence from GMM tests of consumption-based asset-pricing models in Chapter 3. Before reviewing the data, however, it is important to explore in more depth the restrictions that GMM tests attempt to uncover.

Consider two securities, a riskfree asset, and some risky security n. Start from the unconditional version of the moment conditions, (2.19), and rewrite them in terms of covariances (analogous to the way we derived the general asset-pricing model in (1.34)). For the riskfree rate, R_F:

$$E\left[\frac{1}{R_F}\right] = \delta E\left[\left(\frac{c_A'}{c_A}\right)^\gamma\right]. \qquad [2.21]$$

For the return on the risky security, R_n:

$$E[R_n - R_F] = -\text{cov}\left(\delta\left(\frac{c_A'}{c_A}\right)^\gamma, R_n\right) E\left[\frac{1}{R_F}\right]^{-1}. \qquad [2.22]$$

These two equations lead to the following observations:

1. If consumption growth is fairly constant, $E[(c_A'/c_A)^\gamma]$ and $E[c_A'/c_A]^\gamma$ will be approximately the same. If, in addition, consumption growth is high, $E[c_A'/c_A]^\gamma$ will be low, and hence, the average pure discount bond price, $E[1/R_F]$, must be low as well. If the latter is counterfactual (it is), then our consumption-based asset-pricing model can fit the data only by choosing $\delta > 1$, contrary to one of the assumptions with which we started the entire analysis

(see (1.1)). One way to rescue the model is to set γ to a very high absolute value, so that Jensen's inequality bites, driving a wedge between $E[(c'_A/c_A)^\gamma]$ and $E[c'_A/c_A]^\gamma$.

2. To generate a high risk premium $E[R_n - R_F]$, the covariance between consumption growth c'_A/c_A and excess returns $R_n - R_F$ must be high. If it is not (as in the data), then a high risk premium can be reconciled with the model only if γ is chosen to be large as well.

So, on both accounts, the consumption model can fit data with steady consumption growth, low riskfree rates and high risk premiums only if γ is allowed to be high in absolute value. As we will discuss in the next chapter, this is precisely what happens in the U.S. economic data. The situation has become known as the *equity premium puzzle* and was first discovered in Mehra and Prescott (1985). Of course, this is a puzzle only if the values of γ that fit the data are considered to be exorbitant.

2.7 Diagnostics: Variance Bounds

It is possible to formalize the heuristic arguments about the values of the parameters needed to fit a set of return data, given the mean and volatility of aggregate consumption growth. The formalization generates a dramatic visual representation of the potential problems alluded to at the end of the previous section.

The construction was first suggested in Hansen and Jagannathan (1991). We start from the stochastic Euler equations that characterize consumption-based asset-pricing models:

$$\delta E\left[\frac{\frac{\partial \tilde{u}(c'_A)}{\partial c'}}{\frac{\partial \tilde{u}(c_A)}{\partial c}} R_n | x\right] = 1,$$

for all n. To simplify notation, substitute A for the marginal rate of substitution of consumption, as in (1.34):

$$A = \delta \frac{\frac{\partial \tilde{u}(c'_A)}{\partial c'}}{\frac{\partial \tilde{u}(c_A)}{\partial c}}.$$

A will be referred to as the measure of aggregate risk. The stochastic Euler equations become:

$$E[AR_n|x] = 1. \qquad\qquad [2.23]$$

Choose a candidate for A. As in the previous section, we take

$$A = \delta \left(\frac{c_A'}{c_A} \right)^\gamma, \qquad\qquad [2.24]$$

for particular choices of δ and γ. We wish to know whether our candidate A is going to fit the data.

Let r^N denote the vector with the returns on N securities:

$$r^N = \begin{bmatrix} R_1 \\ \cdots \\ R_N \end{bmatrix}.$$

Construct an *estimate of the aggregate risk* $\hat{A}$ as a linear combination of the elements of r^N:

$$\hat{A} = \theta^T r^N.$$

The vector of coefficients θ is chosen so that the estimate of the aggregate risk satisfies the stochastic Euler equations for the N securities returns, (2.23):

$$E\left[\hat{A} R_n | x \right] = E\left[\theta^T r^N R_n | x \right] = 1,$$

for all n. This is a system of N equations and N unknowns. In matrix form:

$$E\left[r^N (r^N)^T | x \right] \theta = \hat{1},$$

where $\hat{1}$ denotes a vector of ones. The solution is:

$$\theta = E\left[r^N (r^N)^T | x \right]^{-1} \hat{1}.$$

If one of the securities is riskfree, with a return R_F, then obviously:

$$E\left[\hat{A} | x \right] = \frac{1}{R_F}.$$

Hence, the expected value of $\hat{A}$ is fixed by the riskfree rate. If no riskfree security exists, we can introduce a dummy riskfree rate R_F^d and add it to the list of security returns. The dummy riskfree rate is chosen to be consistent with the candidate A. In particular:

$$\frac{1}{R_F^d} = E[A|x].$$

By adding R_F^d to r^N, we ensure that the same equation is true for $\hat{A}$:

$$E\left[\hat{A}|x\right] = \frac{1}{R_F^d}.$$

How does $\hat{A}$ provide an indication of the likely fit of A? We write:

$$A = \hat{A} + \xi.$$

Notice two properties of the error ξ:

1. $E[\xi|x] = 0$, because

$$E[\xi|x] = E[A|x] - E[\hat{A}|x] = \frac{1}{R_F^d} - \frac{1}{R_F^d} = 0,$$

by construction.

2. $E[\xi\hat{A}|x] = 0$, again by construction:

$$
\begin{aligned}
E\left[\xi\hat{A}|x\right] &= E\left[\left(A - \hat{A}\right)\left(r^N\right)^T |x\right]\theta \\
&= \left(E\left[A\left(r^N\right)^T |x\right] - E\left[\hat{A}\left(r^N\right)^T |x\right]\right)\theta \\
&= \left(\hat{1}^T - \hat{1}^T\right)\theta \\
&= 0.
\end{aligned}
$$

These two properties imply the following:

$$\boxed{\mathrm{var}(A|x) \geq \mathrm{var}(\hat{A}|x).} \qquad [2.25]$$

That is, the variance of $\hat{A}$ provides a lower bound for the variance of A. The bound has become known as the *Hansen-Jagannathan bound*.

Practically, the Hansen-Jagannathan bound (2.25) provides an easily computable lower bound to the variance of A. If the variance of a candidate for A is below the lower bound, the asset-pricing model it induces, namely, (2.23), is unlikely to fit the data. The lower bound is readily derived from a history of returns on a cross-section of securities. In Chapter 3, we illustrate the technique of deriving the lower bound.

As with GMM tests of consumption-based asset-pricing models, the Hansen-Jagannathan bounds are robust to deletion of part or all of the elements in the state vector x. This should be obvious: (2.23) still obtains after taking expectations of both sides. That is, the unconditional version of (2.23) is formally the same as the conditional version:

$$E[AR_n] = 1.$$

The derivation of the unconditional Hansen-Jagannathan bound is identical to the original one, after deletion of the conditioning vector x.

Likewise, instruments can readily be introduced in the analysis. For instance, take an element x_b from x and multiply both sides of (2.23) by x_b:

$$E[AR_n x_b | x] = x_b.$$

Then take the expectation of both sides:

$$E[AR_n x_b] = E[x_b]. \tag{2.26}$$

The reader is asked to verify, as an exercise, that the variance of the following estimate of A provides a lower bound to the variance of A:

$$\hat{A} = \theta_{x_b}^T r^N, \tag{*}$$

where

$$\theta_{x_b} = E\left[x_b r^N (r^N)^T\right]^{-1} \hat{1} E[x_b].$$

We have covered enough methodology to start evaluating the empirical evidence on asset-pricing theory from historical financial data. Let us do so next.

Exercises

1. Using the numerical data in section 2.3, compute:
   (a) The probabilities of end-of-year outcomes (payoffs on the market and security n, based on combinations of $s_{M,t}$, $\theta_{M,t}$, $s_{n,t}$ and $\theta_{n,t}$), conditional on signals at the end of January ($s_{M,t}$ and $s_{n,t}$);
   (b) Resulting prices of security n and a one-period pure discount bond, at the end of January, based on Rubinstein's model (see (2.5));
   (c) From (b), prices for security n and a one-period pure discount bond, at the beginning of January, also based on Rubinstein's model (see (2.4));

(d) Expected returns in excess of the riskfree rate over both January and the rest of the year;

(e) Covariances of excess returns with aggregate risk, over both January and the rest of the year.

2. Using the same data, now compute:

(a) The probabilities of end-of-year outcomes (payoffs on the market and security n, based on combinations of $s_{M,t}$, $\theta_{M,t}$, $s_{n,t}$ and $\theta_{n,t}$), *conditional* on signals at the end of January ($s_{M,t}$ and $s_{n,t}$) *and* $\theta_{n,t} = 1$;

(b) The probabilities of end-of-January outcomes (combinations of $s_{M,t}$ and $s_{n,t}$), conditional on $\theta_{n,t} = 1$;

(c) Expected returns in excess of the riskfree rate over both January and the rest of the year, conditional on $\theta_{n,t} = 1$;

(d) Covariances of excess returns with aggregate risk, over both January and the rest of the year, conditional on $\theta_{n,t} = 1$.

Now compare the conditional expected excess returns and covariances with your answers for the previous question. Are they the same as the expected excess returns and covariances computed without conditioning on $\theta_{n,t} = 1$?

3. Explain how the finding mentioned in footnote 15 on page 55 could also be the result of a subtle selection bias. (*Hint:* Think about what would happen if earnings announcements also signal the very fact that the firm is still in business [i.e., has not yet defaulted]).

4. Does the Hansen-Jagannathan bound (2.25) become stricter as one adds assets in the computation of $\hat{A}$?

5. Prove that the variance of $\hat{A}$ in (*) provides a lower bound to the variance of A.

CHAPTER 3

The Empirical Evidence in a Nutshell

3.1 Introduction

Rather than an encyclopedic account of the numerous empirical studies of asset-pricing theory, this chapter is primarily an anthology. Enough material will be presented for the reader to get a comprehensive view of what has been tried, and how the empirical studies have produced a mixed result at best.

Virtually the entire empirical literature gathers evidence from econometric analysis of historical data from field markets. The reader who is unfamiliar with finance research may not appreciate how difficult it is to test theory on historical field data. Many auxiliary assumptions must be made for the inference to be valid. In tests of asset-pricing theory, a measure of aggregate risk must be chosen. A decision about investors' beliefs must be made, which, as discussed in Chapter 2, has invariably been that investors have unbiased beliefs. To determine the sampling properties of the statistics used to determine the validity of the theory, certain assumptions about the data-generating process are made. These assumptions can include stationarity.

The complexity of inference from historical data should be kept in mind if, by the end of this chapter, the reader has become pessimistic about the scientific validity of asset-pricing theory. Understandably, the empirical studies to date have led many economists to reject asset-pricing theory altogether.

Our anthology starts with empirical analyses of the Capital Asset-Pricing Model (CAPM). Subsequently, evidence on consumption-based models from variance bounds tests will be presented. Third, GMM tests of consumption-based asset-pricing models will be discussed. Finally, we turn to cross-sectional studies, which, as pointed out in Chapter 2, do not rely on one of the pillars of efficient markets hypothesis (EMH), namely, stationarity.

3.2   Empirical Evidence on the CAPM

In conjunction with EMH, asset-pricing theory predicts that average excess returns should be proportional to the conditional covariance with aggregate risk. See (2.2), which is repeated here for ease of reference (the riskfree rate is put inside the expectation on the left hand side):

$$E[R_n - R_F|x] = -\text{cov}\left(\frac{A}{E[A|x]}, R_n|x\right).$$

In the CAPM, this boils down to the restriction that average excess returns be proportional to the beta of the market portfolio:

$$E[R_n - R_F|x] = \beta_{n,x}^M E[R_M - R_F|x].$$

We will only consider the unconditional version of the CAPM. That is, we assume that the CAPM obtains unconditionally, as in (2.13), also repeated here:

$$E[R_n - R_F] = \beta_n^M E[R_M - R_F]. \tag{3.1}$$

EMH allows us to estimate the expectations as time-series averages, and to estimate betas (risks) as least squares (LS) slopes in time-series projections of individual asset excess returns onto those of the market portfolio. We look at the simplest graphical evidence by plotting time-series average excess returns against estimated betas.

Although we will look at U.S. stock market data exclusively, the phenomena that we focus on appear to be common to most Western stock markets. We will not consider options, futures, or bond markets. Even if the CAPM were to hold for these markets as well, our assumption that beta does not vary with the state vector x becomes untenable. For instance, the beta for call options changes nonlinearly with moneyness (ratio of strike price over the price of the underlying security).

The most dramatic way to present the evidence on the CAPM is by reproducing some of the results in Fama and French (1992). The data are monthly returns on stock traded on the NYSE, AMEX and NASDAQ, covering the period from July 1963 to December 1990. Stock is first ranked according to size (market capitalization) at the beginning of each year, then grouped in ten decile portfolios. These ten decile portfolios are tracked over the entire period: average monthly returns and betas are estimated. Each month, stock in a decile portfolio is subsequently ranked according to the beta over the previous five years, and then grouped into ten beta-based portfolios. This process produces one hundred size- and beta-based portfolios. Average monthly returns and betas are estimated over the entire sample and plotted. All betas are estimated with respect to the return on the value-weighted index of the Center for Research in Securities Prices (CRSP) of the University of Chicago, a standard "proxy" of the market portfolio.

In Fig. 3.1, average monthly returns on the ten size-based portfolios are plotted against their betas. The positive, proportional relationship between the average monthly returns and beta is striking. The average one-month riskfree rate was one order of magnitude smaller than the average returns on the size-based stock portfolios. Hence, the positive, proportional relationship holds for average *excess* returns as well. This amounts to magnificent support for the CAPM.

Matters look far less convincing when taking a closer look at the data. Take, for instance, the portfolio of stock in the smallest firms (those in the lowest decile), which simultaneously experienced the highest average monthly returns and beta values over the entire sample period. If we split this portfolio into ten beta-based subportfolios and plot their monthly average excess returns against betas, as done in Fig. 3.2,[16] proportionality is completely lost. Moreover, the relationship between average monthly return and beta is now *negative*. The slope is not significantly negative, but the lack of proportionality is highly significant.

16. Only nine beta-based subportfolios are apparent; two had indistinguishable mean returns and beta.

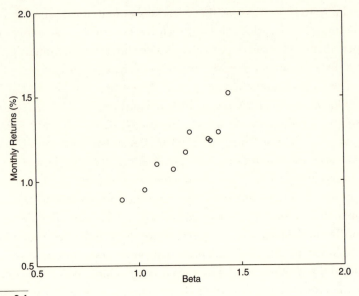

Figure 3.1

CAPM evidence: size-sorted portfolios of U.S. stock, July 1962 to
December 1990.

One could object that small firms are somehow different. In particular, liquidity of small firm stock is notoriously low. This creates measurement problems (synchrony between market returns and individual stock
returns is lost), and one can argue that such stock is really outside the
realm of "investable securities," that is, they are not normally considered
part of an investor's standard portfolio universe.

One can try to tackle measurement problems by using sophisticated
econometric means (e.g., Cohen et al. [1983]), or accommodating a liquidity premium (e.g., Brennan, Chordia, and Subrahmanyam [1998]).
But the simplest way to ascertain whether our finding for small firms is
not caused by the smallness of the issues is to look at large firms. Stock
in large firms is liquid, and hence, should neither cause measurement
problems nor exhibit liquidity premiums. If large firm stock displays similar problems, then there is something genuinely wrong with the CAPM
or EMH.

Figure 3.3 plots average monthly returns and betas of the ten beta-
based subportfolios formed by ranking component stock of the largest

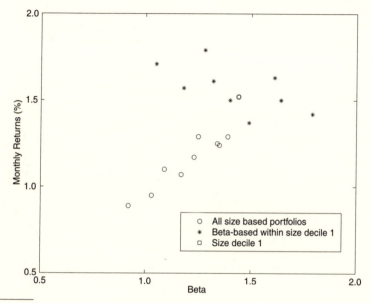

Figure 3.2

CAPM evidence: size-sorted and beta-sorted portfolios of U.S. stock, July 1962 to December 1990. Beta-based within size decile 1.

size decile portfolio. As with small firms, proportionality is lost, and the relationship is negative. As a matter of fact, there is not much difference between this result and that for small firm stock; only a small translation toward zero average returns and beta.

The problem is endemic. Figure 3.4 plots average monthly returns and beta values for the ten beta-based subportfolios of each of the remaining size-based decile portfolios. The slope of the relationship is at best zero; proportionality never obtains.

The formal statistical evidence on the basis of the Fama-MacBeth procedure is no different, even if it allows both average returns and beta to change over time (in the figures, average returns and beta are computed over the entire sampling period—July 1962 to December 1990—thereby assuming that mean returns and beta remain constant). Altogether, the average correlation between the monthly returns on the one hundred size-beta portfolios and their beta values (estimated over the previous five years) is insignificantly different from zero (see Fama and French [1992] for details).

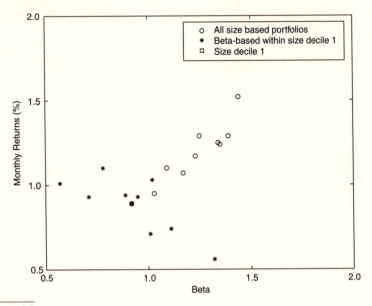

Figure 3.3

CAPM evidence: size-sorted and beta-sorted portfolios of U.S. stock, July 1962 to December 1990. Beta-based within size decile 10.

What can we conclude from this evidence? If the market portfolio can indeed be identified by the value-weighted CRSP index, then the CAPM, together with EMH, must be rejected as a model of pricing in U.S. stock markets.

A more benign conclusion takes into account Roll's critique, discussed in Chapter 1, that conclusive evidence on the CAPM requires that one observe the market portfolio and not a proxy. In our case, the only conclusion we can really draw is that the value-weighted CRSP index was not mean-variance optimal over the period July 1962 to December 1990, for otherwise (3.1) must hold. This only means that it was not optimal for an investor using quadratic utility to have held some combination of the value-weighted CRSP index and the one-month riskfree security. Such a conclusion is not insignificant, given the rising popularity of index funds in professional investment circles. But it says nothing about the validity of the prototype asset-pricing model, the CAPM.

Because of Roll's critique, there have been extensive efforts to investigate how sensitive one's conclusions are to the choice of market proxy.

Within the class of widely traded securities, the conclusions appear to be insensitive (Stambaugh [1982]); when including such nontraded wealth as human capital, the conclusions can change dramatically (Jagannathan and Whang [1996]).

Practical applications of the CAPM almost invariably use proxies that include only widely traded securities. Like the CRSP value-weighted index, such proxies have generally been found to be mean-variance suboptimal, and hence, lead one to reject the CAPM. This presents a puzzle. The use of the CAPM is widespread for matters as diverse as capital budgeting and portfolio performance evaluation. Yet, with the market proxy that is being used, the CAPM should be rejected. Why does the financial community insist on using a model for which it has failed to produce scientific evidence? Mathematical beauty and forceful logic cannot be sufficient reason.

As mentioned when discussing the Roll critique in Chapter 1, one can exploit the fact that (3.1) obtains for any unconditionally mean-variance optimal portfolio. If a portfolio or combination of portfolios be found such that (3.1) holds, then this portfolio in conjunction with (3.1) can be used as an asset-pricing model. But notice that the economic content of such an asset-pricing model may be limited. Excluding arbitrage opportunities, a nontrivial mean-variance trade-off exists, and hence, mean-variance optimal portfolios must obtain, whether financial markets are in equilibrium or not. One may merely be exploiting a mathematical fact to summarize the data. From an economic point of view, the result may only mean that there are no arbitrage opportunities.

This approach has been popular recently, and did lead to the identification of a portfolio that has historically been closer to the mean-variance efficient frontier. It consists of (1) a standard value-weighted market index, (2) an index long in stock of firms with high book value to market value, short in stock of firms with low book value to market value, (3) an index long in stock in small firms, and short in stock in large firms, (4) a momentum index, long in recent winners, and short in recent losers (see, e.g., Fama and French [1996], and Daniel and Titman [1997]).

It is not immediately clear why the portfolio of these indices "works," although Cochrane (1999) provides some ideas, and Berk, Green, and Naik (1999) construct a formal model. Recent evidence suggests that the composition of the portfolio has been changing, casting doubt on the external validity of the finding—see the discussion in Cochrane (1999).

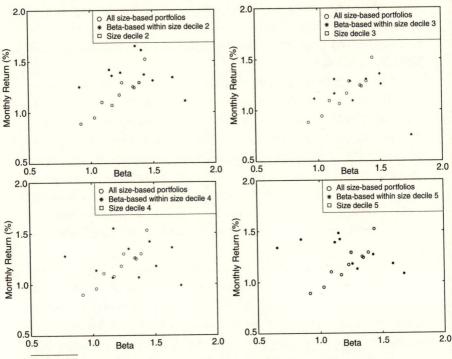

Figure 3.4

CAPM evidence: size-sorted and beta-sorted portfolios of U.S. stock, July 1962 to December 1990. Beta-based within size deciles 2–9.

Moreover, the weights on the indices are even different across countries during the same time period (Hawawini and Keim [1998]). Confirming the suspicion that this line of research exploits mathematical facts, Berk (1995) argues that two pieces of the portfolio, (2) and (3), exploit the fact that market capitalization (share price times number of shares) is highly correlated with average returns, and that this correlation is to be expected, even in the absence of any economic forces.

That market capitalization is highly correlated with average returns should be apparent from Fig. 3.1 and the figures following it: the average return on small firms (the lowest decile) is highest (they also have the highest beta); as we move up the deciles toward the biggest firms (the highest decile), average returns decrease gradually (as do betas). On the face of it, one theory does seem to work: market capitalization matters; or "small is beautiful" (the investor makes most money on small firms). Why this is to be expected even in the absence of any economics is

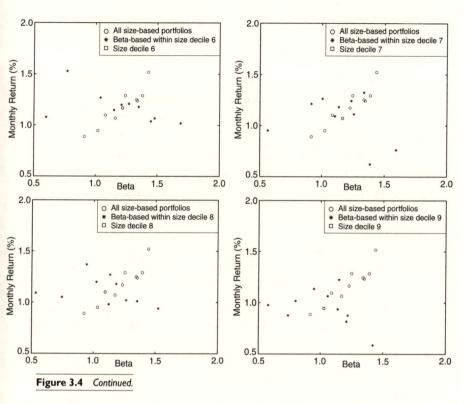

Figure 3.4 *Continued.*

explained as follows. Assume that all firms have the same expected end-of-period prices. They may also differ in terms of risk (deviations from expected end-of-period prices). Suppose that the market prices these firms differently somehow. It is not necessary that there is any price-theoretic consideration behind these differences: only the existence of differences is significant.

It is straightforward to see that these differences cause expected returns on low-priced firms to be highest and expected returns on high-priced firms to be lowest. That is, a size effect is generated. Why? Because expected returns are computed from the ratio of expected end-of-period prices and beginning-of-period prices (we ignore any dividends). The numerator is the same for all firms, whereas the denominator is smaller for small (low-priced) firms.

The argument is not entirely tight, because we never observe expected end-of-period prices, but only realizations (even under EMH).

The Exercises explore a framework in which one does obtain cross-sectional correlation even between prices and realized returns. The assumption that expected end-of-period prices are equal across firms is not needed. But prices have to be set in arbitrary ways relative to realized end-of-period prices, which is quite objectionable. In fact, if past and future prices are sufficiently positively correlated in cross-section, the size effect will disappear altogether.

This qualification does not reduce the importance of the argument. The concern is that a size effect will turn up whenever there is no systematic relationship between today's prices and tomorrow's payoffs. That is, a size effect follows if there is no economics behind pricing.

The fourth component of the portfolio that has historically been closer to the mean-variance efficient frontier is the momentum index. This is a portfolio that invests in recent winners and shorts recent losers. It will generate significant returns if recent winners indeed continue to be winners in the near future, and recent losers continue to be losers. Although added only recently, the presence of the momentum index should not be surprising. It is a residual component, catching all the cross-sectional disparities in mean returns that were left unexplained. Indeed, the expected returns on a momentum index are determined directly by the spread (i.e., variance) of mean returns in cross-section.

To see this, assume that the world is static, in the sense of tests of the CAPM. That is, consider only unconditional expectations and assume that returns are independently and identically distributed over time. Let μ_n denote the expected return on asset n: $\mu_n = E[R_n]$. Define the momentum portfolio for the period between t and $t+1$ as follows. The weight on security n is $(R_{n,t} - R_{E,t})/N$, where $R_{E,t}$ is the previous-period return on an equally weighted portfolio of all securities. That is, security n receives a weight proportional to how much it outperformed an equally-weighted index in the previous period. Because

$$\sum_{n=1}^{N} (R_{n,t} - R_{E,t})/N = \left(\frac{1}{N} \sum_{n=1}^{N} R_{n,t} \right) - R_{E,t}$$
$$= R_{E,t} - R_{E,t}$$
$$= 0,$$

this is a zero-investment portfolio (i.e., the weights add up to zero). The weights are interpreted as number of dollars invested in each security.

Next period's dollar payoff on the momentum index, R_t^{mom}, will be:

$$R_t^{mom} = \sum_{n=1}^{N} (R_{n,t} - R_{M,t}) R_{n,t+1}/N.$$

The expected payoff is:

$$E\left[R_t^{mom}\right] = E\left[\frac{1}{N} \sum_{n=1}^{N} (R_{n,t} - R_{E,t}) R_{n,t+1}\right]$$

$$= E\left[\frac{1}{N} \sum_{n=1}^{N} (R_{n,t} - R_{E,t})(R_{n,t+1} - \mu_n)\right]$$

$$+ E\left[\frac{1}{N} \sum_{n=1}^{N} (R_{n,t} - R_{E,t})\mu_n\right]$$

$$= \frac{1}{N} \sum_{n=1}^{N} \mu_n^2 - E[R_{E,t}]\frac{1}{N} \sum_{n=1}^{N} \mu_n$$

$$= \frac{1}{N} \sum_{n=1}^{N} \mu_n^2 - \left(\frac{1}{N} \sum_{n=1}^{N} \mu_n\right)^2$$

$$> 0.$$

Consequently, the expected payoff equals the cross-sectional variance of mean returns. If there is any difference in mean returns across securities, the momentum index must generate a positive payoff on average. In this sense, the substantial payoffs that momentum portfolios have generated historically prove indirectly that there are significant differences in mean returns.

If differences in expected returns across securities are caused by differences in risk, then of course the profitability of the momentum index merely reflects the fact that one sells (or shorts) low-risk securities and buys high-risk securities. That is, the momentum index exploits risk differentials and must be considered extremely risky. To avoid the risk, one could define the momentum portfolio differently. Let μ_n^e denote the expected return on security n predicted by one's favorite asset-pricing model (e.g., the CAPM). Let ξ_n denote the pricing error of the model:

$$\xi_n = \mu_n - \mu_n^e.$$

Assume that one's favorite asset-pricing model prices securities correctly on average only:

$$\frac{1}{N} \sum_{n=1}^{N} \xi_n = 0.$$

The following momentum portfolio exploits these pricing errors. Define the weight on security n to be

$$(R_{n,t} - \mu_n^e)/N. \qquad [3.2]$$

The resulting index is not a zero-investment portfolio, but the sum of its weights does equal zero on average (the reader is asked to prove this in the Exercises).

Now compute its expected payoff in excess of what the asset-pricing model predicts:

$$E\left[\sum_{n=1}^{N}(R_{n,t} - \mu_n^e)R_{n,t+1}/N\right] - E\left[\sum_{n=1}^{N}(R_{n,t} - \mu_n^e)\mu_n^e/N\right]$$

$$= E\left[\frac{1}{N}\sum_{n=1}^{N}(R_{n,t} - \mu_n^e)(R_{n,t+1} - \mu_n)\right] + E\left[\frac{1}{N}\sum_{n=1}^{N}(R_{n,t} - \mu_n^e)\xi_n\right]$$

$$= E\left[\frac{1}{N}\sum_{n=1}^{N}(R_{n,t} - \mu_n)\xi_n\right] + E\left[\frac{1}{N}\sum_{n=1}^{N}(\xi_n)^2\right]$$

$$= E\left[\frac{1}{N}\sum_{n=1}^{N}(\xi_n)^2\right]$$

$$> 0.$$

The implication is clear: the bigger the mispricing of the asset-pricing model, the greater the outperformance of the momentum index.

The foregoing demonstrates not only that significant returns on momentum portfolios are to be expected, but also that they can be used as a diagnostic test for asset-pricing models. That is, payoffs on momentum indices can be used as the basis of specification tests.

Do consumption-based asset-pricing models fare any better than the CAPM? Let us now turn to this question. First consider whether the measures of aggregate risk that U.S. aggregate consumption generates satisfy the Hansen-Jagannathan variance bounds.

3.3   Hansen-Jagannathan Bounds

Recall the construction of the Hansen-Jagannathan bounds in the previous chapter: we estimate a proxy for aggregate risk, $\hat{A}$, as a linear combination of returns on various securities, compute its variance, and compare this to the variance of the candidate for aggregate risk, A, which we obtain as some transformation of aggregate consumption.

The evidence in Hansen and Jagannathan (1991) is based on a candidate of aggregate risk based on power utility and monthly growth of U.S. aggregate consumption of nondurables and services. Specifically:

$$A = \delta \left(\frac{c_A'}{c_A} \right)^{\gamma},$$

where c_A'/c_A denotes consumption growth. Hansen and Jagannathan (1991) use the one-month U.S. Treasury bill return as well as the monthly return on the CRSP value-weighted index of NYSE stock to construct $\hat{A}$. All data are deflated using the implicit price deflator in the consumption of nondurables and services. The data cover the period March 1959 to December 1986.

As explained in Chapter 2, the Hansen-Jagannathan bounds can also be computed using instruments (referred to as x_b in the previous chapter). In particular, the following four instruments were chosen by Hansen and Jagannathan (1991): the unit constant, the lagged one-month U.S. Treasury bill return, the lagged monthly return on the CRSP value-weighted index of NYSE stock, and lagged consumption growth. Let us discuss the results.

The solid line in Fig. 3.5 depicts the Hansen-Jagannathan lower bound in terms of standard deviation (not variance): it gives the standard deviation of $\hat{A}$ for a range of possible mean values for $\hat{A}$ (the mean will have to be matched with the mean of A). Then, for γ ranging from -1 to -9, and with $\delta = 1$, the resulting combinations of the actual mean of A and standard deviation of A are plotted. In all cases, these combinations are far below the Hansen-Jagannathan bound. Consequently, this diagnostic reveals that it is difficult to fit consumption-based asset-pricing theory with power utility to U.S. securities data.

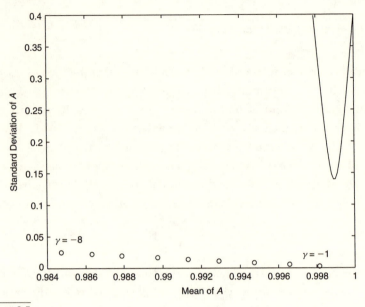

Figure 3.5

Hansen-Jagannathan bound tests for U.S. data, March 1959 to December 1986, for aggregate risk measures based on power utility with $\delta = 1$ and various values of γ. Solid line depicts bound. Circles depict measures of aggregate risk.

As discussed in Chapter 2, the low volatility and high average growth rate of U.S. consumption is to blame for this difficulty. The theory fits the data only by choosing γ with very high absolute value. That may not be apparent from Fig. 3.5, where the situation seems to get worse as γ increases in absolute value, but eventually, for very high values of $|\gamma|$ (greater than 100), we move above the bound. Many consider the resulting values of $|\gamma|$ to be implausibly high.

One can reach the lower bounds much faster (for $|\gamma|$ just greater than 13) by a minor change in the preferences. In particular, let future-period utility be a function of both future and past consumption. In the notation of Chapter 1:

$$u(x', y') = \frac{(x_1' - y' + \lambda x_s')^{\gamma+1}}{\gamma + 1},$$

where x_1' denotes future wealth before consumption, y' denotes future wealth after consumption (the control), and x_s is a state variable with transition equation:

$$x'_s = x_1 - y.$$

We discussed such preferences in Chapter 1; they constitute a simple way of overcoming time separability in standard preferences. When $\lambda < 0$, consumption is intertemporally complementary; this situation is called habit persistence.

These time nonseparable preferences generate the asset-pricing model in (1.38), which we repeat here for convenience:

$$E[AR_n|x] = 1,$$

with

$$A = \delta \frac{(z'_A)^\gamma + \delta\lambda E[(z''_A)^\gamma|x']}{z_A^\gamma + \delta\lambda E[(z'_A)^\gamma|x]}. \qquad [3.3]$$

The computation of A is far more involved: it involves estimating conditional expectations. Hansen and Jagannathan (1991) computed A and its standard deviation for $\lambda = -0.5$ and various values of γ (δ

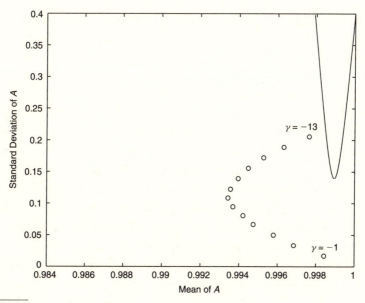

Figure 3.6

Hansen-Jagannathan bound tests for U.S. data, March 1959 to December 1986, for aggregate risk measures based on power utility with habit persistence; $\delta = 1$, $\lambda = -0.5$, and γ varies from -1 to -13. Solid line depicts bound. Circles depict measures of aggregate risk.

was set equal to 1). Figure 3.6 plots the results. Notice that the Hansen-Jagannathan bound is approached as γ increases in absolute value. It is reached for γ just less than -13. Some still find this value too high (in absolute terms), but it is a major improvement over the case with time-separable power utility (Fig. 3.5).

Finance academics often express their reservations about the quality of aggregate consumption data, however. Not only are the data periodically revised, but they are also filtered for seasonality (which is not part of the theory). Instead of joining the debate about the quality of consumption data, one can investigate a particular case, nested among the above cases, where consumption data are not needed. This is Rubinstein's model. It obtains for power utility with $\gamma = -1$ (logarithmic utility) (see Chapter 1).

In Rubinstein's case, A is readily measured by the inverse return on the market portfolio (see also (1.33)):

$$A = \frac{1}{R_M}.$$

Hansen and Jagannathan (1991) plotted the mean and standard deviation of A for Rubinstein's model. The CRSP value-weighted NYSE index was used as proxy for the market portfolio. The result is reproduced in Fig. 3.7. For comparison, the mean and standard deviation of A based on U.S. aggregate consumption data and power utility with $\gamma = -1$ is also plotted.

Notice that A for the consumption-based model with $\gamma = -1$ plots below, but close to the A in the Rubinstein model. (Closeness is measured with respect to the distance from the Hansen-Jagannathan bound.) Hence, there seems to be little difference in the inference we draw from the suspicious aggregate consumption data or from supposedly high-quality financial market data. We will come back to this point later on: there is more to this observation than meets the eye.

So far, however, we have not taken into account sampling error in our estimates of the mean and standard deviation of A or in the estimation of $\hat{A}$ and its standard deviation. The question arises: is the distance between the Hansen-Jagannathan lower bound and the mean–standard deviation locus of a particular A statistically significant?

We can readily answer this for the Rubinstein model. At first sight, it violates the Hansen-Jagannathan bound (see Fig. 3.7). Would our in-

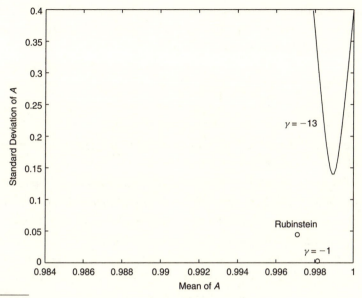

Figure 3.7

Hansen-Jagannathan bound tests for U.S. data, March 1959 to December 1986, for aggregate risk measures based on Rubinstein's model, with the CRSP value-weighted NYSE index proxying for the market portfolio; U.S. consumption data and power utility with $\gamma = -1$. In both cases $\delta = 1$. Solid line depicts bound. Circles depict measures of aggregate risk.

ference change if we take sampling error into account? To evaluate the effect of sampling error, remember that the Hansen-Jagannathan bounds derive from moment conditions. When employing instruments x_b (as in Hansen and Jagannathan [1991]), the moment conditions are given in (2.26). In terms of Rubinstein's model, they become:

$$E\left[\frac{1}{R_M}R_n x_b\right] = E[x_b]. \qquad [3.4]$$

In Hansen and Jagannathan (1991), two securities and four instruments were used. The two securities were: the one-month Treasury bill and the one-month return on the CRSP value weighted NYSE index. Because the latter is also used as market proxy, the corresponding moment conditions are automatically satisfied, because

$$E\left[\frac{1}{R_M}R_M x_b\right] = E[1 x_b] = E[x_b].$$

This means that (3.4) generates only four genuine moment conditions, involving only the riskfree security. We can verify these conditions by computing the following sample average:

$$\frac{1}{T} \sum_{t=1}^{T} \left(\frac{1}{R_{M,t}} R_{F,t} x_{b,t} - x_{b,t} \right),$$

and testing whether the four sample averages this generates are jointly significantly different from zero.

When multiplied by $\sqrt{T}$, and under stationarity and mixing (i.e., short memory) conditions, the above sample averages will satisfy a central limit theorem. This means that they will be jointly normally distributed in large samples. With the asymptotic covariance matrix, we can orthogonalize the scaled sample averages, such that the sum of their squares will be χ^2 distributed in large samples. The number of degrees of freedom will be equal to the number of sample averages, namely, four.

The results of this statistical exercise are reported in Hansen and Jagannathan (1991). The orthogonalized sum of squared, scaled sample averages (i.e., the χ_4^2 statistic) was 4.88, which is close to the expected value of a χ^2 random variable with four degrees of freedom. The p-value is about 0.3. Consequently, one cannot reject the moment conditions on which the Hansen-Jagannathan bounds are based. This also implies that the violations that may be inferred from Fig. 3.7 are not statistically significant.

This implies that one must be very careful in interpreting plots with Hansen-Jagannathan bounds like Fig. 3.7. Sampling error may trivialize seemingly large violations of the bounds. Our statistical exercise also demonstrates that the ultimate proof of the validity of an asset-pricing model must be statistical. This means running a GMM test on the stochastic Euler equations that characterize the equilibrium. This is precisely what we did for the Rubinstein model, and we cannot reject it. Epstein and Zin (1991), and Campbell and Cochrane (1999) also report this for slightly different datasets.

Let us summarize how consumption-based models fare when they are confronted with the formal statistical rigor of GMM tests.

3.4 GMM Tests of Consumption-Based Models

Since Hansen and Singleton (1982), there has been a strong interest in fitting a consumption-based asset-pricing model to U.S. data. Rejections were soon reported, in contrast to the ease with which Rubinstein's model fits the data. Presumably, this is caused by the extremely low volatility of U.S. aggregate consumption growth, which is used to construct the measure of aggregate risk A. Compare this with Rubinstein's model: to compute A, one uses the reciprocal of the market return, which is an order of magnitude more volatile. The impact on the volatility of A is dramatic, as is seen by comparing the vertical distance between the position of A for Rubinstein's model and that for the consumption-based model with $\gamma = -1$ in Fig. 3.7.

Notice that the apparent closeness between Rubinstein's model and the consumption-based model pointed out in Fig. 3.7 is now described as "dramatic." The distance is small relative to either model's distance from the Hansen-Jagannathan bound. But in terms of GMM tests of their respective moment conditions, this distance is highly significant.

It would distract us if we were to summarize the attempts at fitting a consumption-based asset-pricing model to U.S. data after Hansen and Singleton (1982). Recent efforts have focused on preferences with habit persistence. That this condition may provide a better fit is apparent from Fig. 3.6. A nice summary, and, in a certain sense, a culmination of these efforts, can be found in Campbell and Cochrane (1999). The reader who is interested in a comprehensive account of theory and tests of consumption-based models should consult Cochrane (2001).

But a dose of scepticism is needed when interpreting the accomplishments: it took about twenty years to fit a consumption-based model to what turns out to be a very small historical dataset, both over time (about 150 years of annual data, and 50 years of monthly data) and in cross-section (usually only a stock index and a few Treasury securities are included in the analysis).

Here we should discuss certain aspects of the modeling that have not yet been examined closely. In particular, let us elaborate on the fact that empirical studies of consumption-based asset-pricing models generally consider only a small cross-section of securities.

Unlike tests of the CAPM, tests of consumption-based asset-pricing models are almost invariably based on a few securities. Although not the goal of the authors, the results in Chen, Roll, and Ross (1986) can be used to gauge the promise of consumption-based asset-pricing models in explaining the pattern of returns in a larger cross-section of risky securities, namely, twenty value-weighted, size-based portfolios.

In Chen, Roll, and Ross (1986), a consumption beta (i.e., the slope in LS projections of excess returns onto consumption growth) was used as one of the measures to explain the cross-sectional pattern of average excess returns. Although a consumption-beta asset-pricing model can be derived explicitly in the continuous-time world of Itô processes (see Breeden [1979]), second-order expansions also deliver such a model in discrete time, albeit as an approximation.[17] This discrete-time consumption-beta model can then be used to interpret the empirical results in Chen, Roll, and Ross (1986). In particular, estimates of the parameters of the representative consumer's power preferences can be read from the empirical results.

To derive the approximate discrete-time consumption-beta model, we start with our general formulation, (1.34), repeated here for ease of reference (after pulling the riskfree rate inside the expectation on the left-hand side):

$$E[R_n - R_F|x] = -\text{cov}\left(\frac{A}{E[A|x]}, R_n|x\right).$$

Substitute the inverse riskfree rate for $E[A|x]$:

$$\frac{1}{R_F} = E[A|x],$$

so that

$$E[R_n - R_F|x] = -R_F\text{cov}(A, R_n|x).$$

If an aggregate investor with power utility exists, then:

$$A = \delta\left(\frac{c_A'}{c_A}\right)^\gamma.$$

(See (2.24); c_A' and c_A denote present and future aggregate consumption,

17. These quadratic approximations become exact in the limit of continuous time, by Itô's lemma.

respectively.) Remembering that $\gamma < 0$, implement a quadratic approximation of A about $c'_A/c_A = 1$:

$$A = \delta \left(\frac{c'_A}{c_A}\right)^\gamma$$

$$\approx \delta \left[1 + \gamma \left(\frac{c'_A}{c_A} - 1\right) + \tfrac{1}{2}\gamma(\gamma - 1)\left(\frac{c'_A}{c_A} - 1\right)^2\right]$$

$$= \delta \left[1 - |\gamma| \left(\frac{c'_A}{c_A} - 1\right) + \tfrac{1}{2}|\gamma|(1 + |\gamma|)\left(\frac{c'_A}{c_A} - 1\right)^2\right].$$

Plugging this into our general asset-pricing formula leads to:

$$E[R_n - R_F | x]$$

$$\approx \delta|\gamma|R_F \text{cov}\left(\frac{c'_A}{c_A}, R_n | x\right) - \tfrac{1}{2}\delta|\gamma|(1 + |\gamma|)\text{cov}\left(\left(\frac{c'_A}{c_A} - 1\right)^2, R_n | x\right)$$

$$= \delta|\gamma|R_F \text{var}\left(\frac{c'_A}{c_A} | x\right)\beta^C_{n,x} - \tfrac{1}{2}\delta|\gamma|(1 + |\gamma|)\text{cov}\left(\left(\frac{c'_A}{c_A} - 1\right)^2, R_n | x\right),$$

where $\beta^C_{n,x}$ denotes the *consumption beta* (i.e., the slope of a conditional LS projection of R_n onto c'_A/c_A).

We can ignore the second term if:

$$\text{cov}\left(\left(\frac{c'_A}{c_A} - 1\right)^2, R_n | x\right) = 0,$$

which obtains, for instance, when aggregate consumption growth and returns on individual securities are jointly normally distributed. We obtain the following *Consumption-Beta Asset-Pricing Model*:

$$E[R_n - R_F | x] \approx \beta^C_{n,x}\lambda_x, \qquad [3.5]$$

where λ_x, the risk premium, equals:

$$\lambda_x = \delta|\gamma|R_F \text{var}\left(\frac{c'_A}{c_A} | x\right). \qquad [3.6]$$

Notice that the risk premium increases with increasing risk aversion ($|\gamma|$) and volatility of consumption growth, as well as with other variables.

For each year, Chen, Roll, and Ross (1986) report estimates of consumption betas for a cross-section of twenty value-weighted, size-based portfolios of U.S. stock, based on the previous five years. Each month's excess returns are then projected cross-sectionally onto the estimated consumption betas. The intercept should be zero, and the slope should be an estimate of λ_x, a positive risk premium. To evaluate this, Chen, Roll, and Ross (1986) repeat this procedure for every month in the period from January 1964 to December 1984. They report tests on whether the intercept was zero on average, and whether the slope coefficient was positive on average. Notice that this effectively implements the Fama-MacBeth testing method discussed in Chapter 2 in terms of the CAPM.

In principle, the consumption betas should have been estimated conditionally: that is, the projections should have been conditional on the state vector x. In Chen, Roll, and Ross (1986), consumption betas are allowed to vary over time, but the estimates do not fully condition on all available information. As discussed in Chapter 1, full conditioning is necessary because of Jensen's inequality. We discussed this in the context of the CAPM, but the arguments obviously apply to the consumption-beta asset-pricing model as well. In what follows, we will ignore this criticism of the estimates of beta.

For the first step of the Fama-MacBeth procedure the consumption betas used in Chen, Roll, and Ross (1986) are estimated together with additional betas, such as those with respect to the return on a market proxy, or with respect to shocks to industrial production. That is, the first-step projections produced multivariate rather than univariate betas. In contrast, the consumption-beta asset-pricing model in (3.5) is cast in terms of univariate values. Again, we must ignore the resulting complication.

Regarding the second step of the Fama-MacBeth procedure, the results in Chen, Roll, and Ross (1986) are based on projections that include these additional betas as explanatory variables. This way, the results provide a test of the consumption-beta asset-pricing model against the alternative that other betas, and hence, other asset-pricing models do a better job at explaining the cross-sectional patterns of expected excess returns. Chen, Roll, and Ross (1986) argue that the market beta, and hence, the CAPM, did not improve upon some of the other betas. Therefore, the results reported below ignore the market beta.

The results of Chen, Roll, and Ross (1986) are reproduced in Table 3.1. To evaluate the magnitude of the estimated coefficients (risk premiums), it seems that the excess returns were expressed in *percent per year*. Consider first the intercept, which should be zero. Although large in absolute terms, it is always insignificantly different from zero, confirming that average excess returns are proportional to beta. Second, consider

Table 3.1

Estimated Risk Premiums for U.S. Stock Markets, 1964–84

Period	Intercept	Cons	IP	EInfl	UInfl	Default	Term
				Betas[1]			
1964–84	2.29	0.68	15.0	−0.17	−0.85	8.81	−6.91
	(0.63)	(0.11)	(3.8)	(−1.74)	(−2.25)	(2.58)	(−1.79)
1964–77	−1.91	−0.45	18.2	0.17	−0.95	11.4	−9.19
	(−0.44)	(−0.66)	(3.54)	(−2.42)	(−2.49)	(3.29)	(−2.41)
1978–84	10.7	1.17	8.59	−0.17	−0.65	3.56	−2.38
	(1.61)	(1.00)	(1.48)	(−0.66)	(−0.77)	(0.47)	(−0.27)

Source: From Chen, Roll, and Ross (1986). © 1986 by The University of Chicago. All rights reserved.

[1]Cons = U.S. monthly consumption growth; IP = U.S. industrial production growth; EInfl = change in U.S. expected inflation; UInfl = unanticipated U.S. inflation; Default = U.S. default premium (yield on Baa bonds minus yield on Treasuries); Term = unanticipated change in the term premium (yield on long-term Treasuries minus short-term Treasuries). *t*-statistics in parentheses.

the coefficient of the consumption beta. This is the risk premium λ_x, and should be significantly positive. It never is. In the first subperiod (1964–77), it is in fact negative, although insignificant. Instead, risk premiums to other betas are generally significant. But in the second subperiod (1978–84), no risk premium is significant, perhaps because of multicollinearity, or lack of power (this period includes far fewer observations than does the first subperiod).

Despite our finding that the estimate of the risk premium to the consumption beta, λ_x, is insignificant, let us use the estimate for the entire period 1964–84 to extract an estimate of the risk-aversion parameter γ. We are interested in verifying whether the value we obtain through this cross-sectional analysis is equally disturbing as the one we needed to satisfy the Hansen-Jagannathan bounds for consumption-based asset-pricing models.

Epstein and Zin (1991) report that the volatility of monthly consumption growth in the period 1959–86 is about 0.76 percent per month. Let us take δ to be the reciprocal of R_F, so that δR_F equals approximately 1. Although this is not mentioned explicitly, the numbers indicate that Chen, Roll, and Ross (1986) expressed consumption growth as percent per year. If so, the estimate of the risk premium to the consumption beta (λ_x), 0.68, is also expressed in percent per year. From (3.6), an estimate of the consumption beta risk premium equal to 0.68% per year, or 0.057% per month, implies an estimate of

$$\gamma \approx -10,$$

which is much lower than we needed in our analysis of the Hansen-Jagannathan lower bounds, where we used only two securities, a riskfree security and a market index.

This means that the pattern of expected excess returns across twenty value-weighted, size-based portfolios generates an estimate of risk aversion that is far more plausible than when comparing the average return on a market index against that on a riskfree security (i.e., the equity premium).

Of course, the above analysis is made less forceful by the insignificance of the estimated consumption-beta risk premium. In particular, risk neutrality ($\gamma = 0$) cannot be rejected either. As an exercise, the reader is asked to compute the value of γ that corresponds to the upper boundary of the 95% confidence interval of the estimate of the consumption-beta risk premium. This will give an idea of the range of levels of risk aversion that are likely to be consistent with replications of the test on similar data.

Table 3.1 demonstrates that other betas pick up the cross-sectional pattern in average excess returns. It appears that aggregate risk is summarized far better in terms of betas with respect to growth in industrial production, changes in expected inflation and surprises in inflation, changes in the default premium and the term premium, than in terms of either a market beta (i.e., CAPM) or consumption beta (i.e., consumption-based asset-pricing models).

In a certain sense, this is not surprising. The proxies for the market portfolio that we generally use include only equity, which is a small fraction of the total supply of risky securities. Consequently, our market proxies are not very good. Likewise, our measures of aggregate consumption are suspect. It may very well be that some combination of industrial production, inflation, default, and term premiums measures aggregate risk far better than either our market proxies or our aggregate consumption series.

The result is that a model with risk measured as a combination of industrial production, inflation, default, and term premiums works better than a model where risk is measured in terms of market returns or consumption growth. How does this model compare to one where betas are computed with respect to carefully picked portfolios that as a group appear to have been mean-variance efficient historically? We have discussed the latter approach in the context of the CAPM. The two approaches are similar. In particular, both can be criticized for being more data driven than inspired by asset-pricing theory. In Chen, Roll, and Ross (1986), it is a leap of faith to jump from the proposed risk factors to aggregate risk. For instance, it is not clear why the default premium constitutes aggregate risk. The default premium measures the compensation bondholders receive for default risk. Standard theory of corporate finance claims that this risk is perfectly diversifiable (this is the Modigliani-Miller theorem). Hence, it does not exist in the aggregate, and no investor should be compensated for holding it.

Whatever the view one takes, the evidence for asset-pricing theory from historical data is not overwhelming. The complexity of historical studies makes it very hard to pinpoint the problem. Is it asset-pricing theory itself, or the assumptions about beliefs and stationarity (EMH)? Fat tails in return distributions may invalidate the distributional assumptions behind the statistical tests. Or there may be subtle selection biases (e.g., we don't use correct divestment prices for delisted stock). And there are other possible sources of error. We can try to investigate one possibility: violations of stationarity. Stationarity is an integral part of EMH, and EMH is assumed throughout the tests we have discussed so far. In Chapter 2, we showed how inference becomes biased when stationarity is violated. But we also argued that cross-sectional studies are more robust. So let us turn to the cross-sectional studies and see whether they produce more favorable results.

3.5 Cross-Sectional Tests

Figure 3.8 typifies the results from cross-sectional (i.e., event) studies. The case concerns the returns around 143 announcements of U.S. equity repurchase offers in the period 1962–76 (see Dann [1981]). As explained in Chapter 2, the cross-section of return histories is aligned in terms of the number of days relative to the event, namely, the repurchase offer announcement. The positive return from four days before to two days after the event day itself merely represents the effect of the news embed-

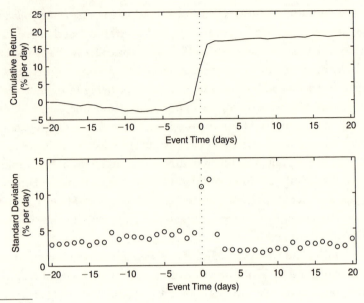

Figure 3.8

Cumulative average daily returns and volatility around 143 announcements of stock repurchase offers in the U.S. in the period 1962–76.

ded in the announcement (see the top panel of Fig. 3.8). Apparently, the stock market favors repurchase offers, perhaps because it increases the leverage of the company, and hence, the value of equity holdings. That the price increase starts before the announcement (it is significant from day −4 on[18]) may reflect news leakage and insider trading. Or it may reflect inaccurate measurement of the actual announcement time. The latter may explain why the average price runup remains significant on days +1 and +2.[19]

We are concerned about how the stock price behaves on average in the days after the seven-day announcement period. We do not see any evidence of predictability, beyond a small, steady rise in the price. The latter could be a risk premium, which is earned gradually over time. The average daily return is 0.11%, which amounts to an annual return of 28% (based on 250 trading days). That is fairly high, but within the normal range of average returns on individual stock.

18. The t-statistics for day −4 equals 2.65.
19. The t-statistics for days +1 and +2 equal 6.77 and 2.54, respectively.

The average return in the period before the seven-day announcement period is negative, namely, -0.16% per day. This, of course, may be the result of selection bias: only firms that announced a repurchase offer were retained in the sample, and the equity of those firms happened to have experienced gradual price decreases, which may have triggered the repurchase announcement: management may have perceived their stock to be undervalued, and hence, decided to repurchase part of it.

To a certain extent, it is puzzling that this gradual price decrease occurs with high cross-sectional volatility. The bottom panel of Fig. 3.8 plots the evolution of the volatility (i.e., standard deviation of the return across securities) in event time. On a "normal day" (i.e., a day after the seven-day announcement period), the volatility is typically 2.6%. This corresponds to an annual volatility of 40%, which is normal for individual stock. Yet, in days before the seven-day announcement period, the volatility is typically 3.6%, which amounts to an annual volatility of 57%. Of course, the higher volatility in the pre-announcement period may be the effect of selection bias: repurchase offers are triggered by a combination of low returns and high volatility.[20]

The bottom panel of Fig. 3.8 also documents that, during the announcement period, volatility increases, up to 12%. This may reflect heterogeneity of the specifics of the repurchase offers (number of securities solicited, repurchase price, etc.), as well as of the ensuing valuation effects (differential effects on leverage, capital gains taxes, etc.).

Although the evidence about asset-pricing theory from such studies as Dann (1981) is in general positive, it is also minimal. The price changes after events may not be predictable beyond a small, steady increase, but one generally does not evaluate whether they are consistent in other re-

---

20. Appealing to the theory presented in Chapter 5, however, Bossaerts (1998) shows that the combination of low returns and high volatility is to be expected in an efficient market: when securities are selected ex post because they did not perform well, then one expects to observe unusually high cross-sectional volatility. Likewise, when securities are picked because they performed well over a certain period, exceptionally high volatility will be recorded as well. This phenomenon can be observed in very different samples. Bossaerts (1998) studies nine-day periods in which the S&P 500 index has done unusually poorly (say, dropped 3%) between 1929 and 1997. The average daily return over the first three days of those nine-day periods was low (of course), but the volatility was invariably exceptionally high. The increase in daily volatility is equally striking for periods when the S&P 500 did extremely well.

spects with asset-pricing theory. In particular, is the average price change proportional to the covariance with aggregate risk?

One study that did evaluate consistency with a specific asset-pricing model is Ibbotson (1975). Specifically, it tested the CAPM on the average price change during each of the first sixty months after U.S. initial public offerings (IPOs) of common stock in the period 1960–69. He found that the CAPM predicted lower average returns than actually recorded in the first five months, and higher average returns than actually recorded in the period from one to four years after the IPO.

A similar, more recent study is Ritter (1991), which is based on 1,526 U.S. IPOs in the period 1975–84. Rather than evaluating the aftermarket performance of the IPOs against a specific model like the CAPM, Ritter (1991) compared it to that of carefully matched (by size and industry) established firms, on the grounds that they should be equally risky, and hence, command the same risk premium.

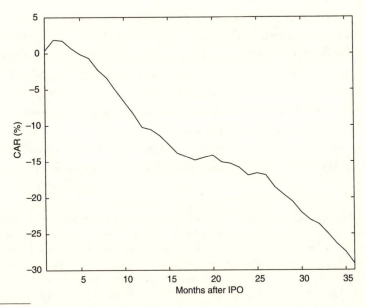

Figure 3.9

Cumulative average monthly returns (CAR) on 1,526 U.S. IPOs in the period 1975–84, in excess of the CAR on equity in established firms matched by size and industry, excluding the first day of trading. Constructed on the basis of Table II in Ritter (1991).

Figure 3.9 plots the cumulative average return (CAR) on these IPOs in excess of that on the matched firms, for thirty-six months after the IPO date. Although standard, a plot of CAR is hard to interpret without accompanying standard errors.[21] Still, the t-statistic of the CAR after thirty-six months, at -5.9, is highly significant. Thus the visual image of dismal performance apparent in Fig. 3.9 is real (i.e., statistically significant).

The evidence in Ibbotson (1975) and Ritter (1991) is damaging for asset-pricing theory. We know that such cross-sectional studies do not rely on stationarity, and hence, are robust to one component of EMH. But other things can go wrong. For instance, these cross-sectional studies are sensitive to violations of the second component of EMH, namely, that market beliefs are correct (see (2.2)).

We could investigate whether the assumption of unbiased market beliefs is at fault. This assumption implies, among other things, that the market's beliefs about default coincide with the actual hazard rates of default (except for the usual sampling error). To do so, however, we need a new testing methodology, introduced in Chapter 5.

Of course, there are other reasons why the results in Ibbotson (1975) and Ritter (1991) are not supportive of asset-pricing theory. But the possibility that the market held biased priors about the chances of default seems plausible. Many IPOs are launched in new industries, or in unfamiliar situations. For instance, the sample we have just discussed contains 127 IPOs in the oil and gas industry, most of which were floated in 1980–81, and a large number of which defaulted in the subsequent surprise decline in the price of crude oil.

Table 3.2 provides details on the fate of U.S. IPOs in the period covered by Ritter (1991). The sample is slightly larger (1,856). In Chapter 6, we follow the IPOs up to five years after the issue, instead of only three; also, we extend the sample to include all IPOs between 1974 and 1995. Table 3.2 documents that a full 10 percent of the IPOs had been liquidated within three years. Ignoring the (miniscule) sampling error, the market's prior should have been identical for EMH to obtain.[22] Similarly,

---

21. Even if the expected excess return is zero, the cumulative (i.e., summed) sample average excess return (CAR) will wander like a random walk.

22. Under EMH, the market's prior should be identical to the true probability of default. Table 3.2 provides an estimate of the latter, namely, 10.7 percent. With a sample of 1,856 observations, the standard error on this estimate is $\sqrt{0.107(1 - 0.107)/1,856}$ (i.e., 0.2 percent). This is very small.

Table 3.2

The Fate of U.S. IPOs after One, Two and Three Years, 1975–84

Reference Point	Categories[1]				
	Active	Mergers	Exchanges	Liquidations	Unknown
One year	1809	10	1	21	15
	(97.5)[2]	(0.5)	(0.1)	(1.1)	(0.8)
Two years	1627	48	7	109	65
	(87.7)	(2.6)	(0.4)	(5.9)	(3.5)
Three years	1442	81	13	199	121
	(77.7)	(4.4)	(0.7)	(10.7)	(6.5)

[1]Categories: (i) *Active* issues: CRSP delisting code (DC) 100; (ii) *Mergers*: DCs 200–203; (iii) *Exchanges*: DCs 300–390; (iv) *Liquidations* (and forced delistings): DCs 550–588, 400 and 700; (v) *Unknown* (and inactive): DCs 500–520.
[2]Numbers in brackets: percentage of total.

the market should have known that about half of those were to be liquidated within two years, but only very few within one year.

Because many IPOs take place in new industries (e.g., biotechnology), or to exploit unusual situations (high oil prices), it is doubtful that the market always holds correct beliefs about the likelihood and timing of bankruptcies. It is reasonable to conjecture that EMH is too strong as an auxiliary assumption when investigating IPO aftermarket pricing. The evidence in Chapter 6, based on a methodology that allows the market to have biases in its beliefs about default, will be far more supportive of asset-pricing theory. The underperformance will disappear entirely, except for low-priced issues. This will confirm our conjecture.

3.6　Conclusion

It is fair to conclude that the predictions of asset-pricing theory have largely been rejected in empirical studies of historical data. The evidence against them from time-series analysis is overwhelming. Although the evidence in cross-sectional studies is generally more favorable, it is minimal, or, where it is not, there are disturbing anomalies. Closer inspection of the latter suggests that lack of stationarity is not to blame. (Remember that EMH, the assumption on which time-series studies of asset pricing are based, requires that the data be stationary.)

At this point, there seem to be at least three possible routes to try to get us out of this disappointing situation.

The first route is to attempt to discover statistical regularities that are common across time periods and/or financial markets, and to develop a theory of finance based on those regularities, even if the fundamental reasons for their existence are not understood. As mentioned before, this appears to be the route that many have recently taken (see, e.g., Davis, Fama, and French [2000]). This path will not be chosen here. One of the goals of this book is to demonstrate that there is no need to become agnostic.

The second one is to develop a testing methodology that relaxes EMH, by allowing markets to have biased beliefs, at least to some extent. This approach is possible without losing many of the attractive features of the existing methodology (robustness and parsimonious use of conditioning information). Chapters 5 and 6 follow this route.

The third route implements a scientist's natural inclination when confronted with an immensely complex field, that is, to try some experiments. The idea is to design simple experimental financial markets where one can identify unambiguously when and how the basic principles of asset-pricing theory emerge. Experimentation would not be the choice for the impatient practitioner, who wants ready answers for pressing problems, because rarely is it immediately clear how success in the laboratory can be extrapolated to the incredibly complex world of financial markets that were obviously not designed to study the theory. Experiments, in contrast, give one the opportunity to isolate the basic principles, and to determine whether these are sound.

Because we urgently need to know whether the basic principles of asset-pricing theory are correct, let us explore some simple experiments in the next chapter.

Exercises

1. Let there be N securities, indexed $n = 1, \ldots, N$. Write security n's end-of-period price as the sum of the cross-sectional expected price $\overline{P}'$ plus an error ϵ'_n:

$$P'_n = \overline{P} + \epsilon'_n.$$

Computing expectations in cross-section, this means: $E[\epsilon'_n] = 0$. The beginning-of-period price P_n is set independently of the error ϵ'_n. (For instance, if N is even, assume that half the securities' prices are arbitrarily set equal to $2, and the other half are set to $0.5.) Now, let R_n denote the period return: $R_n = P'_n/P_n$. Show that:

$$\mathrm{cov}(R_n, P_n) \leq 0,$$

that is, there is a nonpositive cross-sectional association between return and price. (Notice that we do not relate price setting to an explicit asset-pricing model!)

2. Continuing problem 1, show that the correlation between R_n and P_n may become positive if P_n and ϵ'_n are positively correlated (i.e., securities with higher end-of-period prices also sold for a higher price initially).

3. Prove that the portfolio with weights (3.2) is a zero-investment portfolio on average.

4. In Chapter 2, we discussed that Hansen-Jagannathan bounds are valid even if we do not observe the entire information set (the state vector x) on which investors condition their beliefs. We were a bit sloppy there, because whether this is correct depends on the nature of aggregate risk, A. One case where the claim is false is the time nonseparable preferences that lead to the aggregate risk in (3.3). Why is it false in that case? What would the general rule be for the claim to be correct?

5. In Table 3.1, the t-statistic for the consumption risk premium over 1964–84 is 0.11. With a point estimate of 0.68, this means that the high end of the 95% confidence level for the consumption risk premium equals approximately $0.68 + 1.96 \times 0.68/0.11 = 12.8$ percent. Using (3.6), compute the level of risk aversion ($|\gamma|$) that the latter implies.

6. Prove that the variance of post-event one-month CARs like the one plotted in Fig. 3.9 increases linearly in the time since the event, even if the expected return equals zero, and hence, that CARs are really random walks.

CHAPTER 4

The Experimental Evidence

4.1 Introduction

The central prediction of asset-pricing theory is that financial markets equilibrate to the point that expected returns become proportional to the covariance with aggregate risk. See (1.34), which is repeated here for ease of reference (the riskfree rate is pulled inside the conditional expectation):

$$E[R_n - R_F|x] = -\text{cov}\left(\frac{A}{E[A|x]}, R_n|x\right).$$

Specific asset-pricing models give concrete meaning to the notion of aggregate risk. The Capital Asset-Pricing Model (CAPM), for instance, associates aggregate risk with the return on the market portfolio, and the prediction is that expected excess returns are proportional to the beta with the market portfolio:

$$E[R_n - R_F|x] = \beta_{n,x}^M E[R_M - R_F|x].$$

(This is (1.26).) If markets are complete, in the sense that there are as many securities with independent payoff patterns as there are possible states, then the Arrow-Debreu model predicts that the ratio of the prices for two equally likely states w and v is given by the ratio of marginal utilities of consumption of an aggregate investor across the two states:

$$\frac{P_{x,w}}{P_{x,v}} = \frac{\frac{\partial \tilde{u}(c'_{A,w})}{\partial c'}}{\frac{\partial \tilde{u}(c'_{A,v})}{\partial c'}}.$$

(This is (1.35).) Risk aversion (i.e., decreasing marginal utility) then implies that the state prices are ranked inversely with respect to the ranking of aggregate wealth across the states.

These are very precise predictions, but, for a variety of reasons, they do not seem to be supported by the field data.

Many problems can plague tests on field data, however. Tests rely on a host of auxiliary assumptions that are not necessarily part of asset-pricing theory, such as efficient markets hypothesis (EMH). They require that the empiricist observe the return on the market portfolio (in the case of the CAPM) or aggregate wealth (in the case of the Arrow-Debreu model). They assume that the recorded prices are equilibrium prices, and so on.

The list of potential problems is frighteningly long: empirical tests on field data are very challenging. And yet the question lingers: is the problem one of faulty econometric methodology, or is asset-pricing theory itself wrong?

Asset-pricing theory is both elegant and logically compelling. It is a nice piece of applied mathematics. But this is not sufficient to conclude that it has scientific merit. To establish the latter, its predictions need to be verified in a variety of contexts. In particular, the theory should be able to predict the outcomes in simple, experimental financial markets. These markets should equilibrate, to the point that expected excess returns are proportional to covariance with aggregate risk.

As in the natural sciences, economic experiments provide a unique opportunity to evaluate whether and when the predictions of the theory obtain. All theory is merely based on a model of reality. The image of an atom with a nucleus and layers of electrons around it is but an image. We know, among other things, that it is incomplete. Yet its success in predicting the outcomes of simple biochemical reactions is without doubt, because the theoretical results are replicable in experiment.

Similarly, we will demonstrate that asset-pricing theory correctly predicts the direction of price movement in experimental financial markets. This success obtains despite the stylized and abstract nature of asset-pricing theory. The power of the theory lies in its replicability: we are not merely stating that asset-pricing theory explains a particular history of financial markets, but that it can predict outcomes in future experiments of the same kind.

One may think that comparing financial markets experiments with theory is a no-brainer. Either the theory applies, and subjects know the theory and act accordingly; or the theory does not apply, and subjects do not know the theory, and hence, behave unlike the assumptions of the theory. The experiments that we are going to discuss, however, were designed so that subjects do not have the information to act according to the theory, even if they want to. Among other models, we will study the CAPM. If subjects really want to use the CAPM to set prices, they must know the market portfolio. Yet, in the experiments discussed here, they were not given this information and it was virtually impossible for them to infer what the market portfolio was. Consequently, when the CAPM emerged from the experiments, the cause could only have been competitive interaction between risk-averse subjects.

Bear in mind that the predictions of asset-pricing theory are not a foregone conclusion, despite their compelling nature. The theory is based on equilibrium, but it is silent about how to reach equilibrium. We discussed this at the end of Chapter 1. In the context of the CAPM, we presented a simple model of price discovery that predicted that equilibration may fail. Even so, our model was very idealized and ignored many crucial issues. For instance, when there are multiple securities, equilibration requires a high level of coordination. Standard organized exchanges are viewed as parallel markets, with little possibility of coordination, because one cannot submit orders in one market to be executed conditionally on events in other markets. Without sufficient coordination, it is unclear how markets equilibrate.[23]

One may object that experimental markets are not real. It is fine that they are not designed to mimic such field markets as the U.S. NASDAQ. But that is done purposely: the experimental markets should be simple enough to establish unambiguously that the theory is correct. And because they are simple does not mean that they are less real

---

23. Using a market microstructure framework, Wohl and Kandel (1997) demonstrate theoretically that the quality of price discovery indeed increases when orders are introduced that allow agents to coordinate their trades across securities.

than field markets. They are real markets, with real people who trade real money.

Why would we expect asset-pricing theory to be able to predict the outcomes in experimental financial markets? The theory studies the pricing and allocation of risk among risk-averse agents. In the laboratory, risks are small. If subjects' risk attitudes can indeed be described by the expected utility theory on which asset-pricing models are based, then risk neutrality should emerge in the laboratory: risk-neutral pricing without risk sharing. After all, the same subjects are willing to buy into far bigger field risks at much smaller risk premiums!

The disparity between risk-taking in the field and in experimental markets is a legitimate concern only if one views expected utility theory as all-encompassing. According to this view, agents make decisions that are fully consistent over time and scales of risk, no matter how different the circumstances are. But, expected utility theory does not claim to be all-encompassing.[24] In addition, there is ample evidence, both from experiments and from the field, that people are risk averse, but make decisions that are inconsistent over time and scales of risk. That is, the view of an all-encompassing expected utility theory is factually wrong.

So we should keep an open mind about risk aversion in experimental financial markets. Risk aversion does manifest itself. The issue then becomes whether it forces prices in the direction predicted by asset-pricing theory. One can state this differently. How is risk aversion reflected in the aggregate? Does it emerge in pricing as if markets are populated with expected utility maximizers? The answer to the latter question is affirmative.

Experimental verification of asset-pricing theory is a recent endeavor. Only very few economic experiments have ever been attempted that focus on the pricing and allocation of risk. The most important of these experiments are Levy (1997), Bossaerts and Plott (2001), Bossaerts and Plott (1999), Bossaerts, Fine, and Ledyard (2000), and Bossaerts, Plott, and Zame (2000).

This chapter demonstrates that experimental investigation of asset-pricing theory is promising and may help us in understanding the work-

---

24. See the analysis in Rabin (2000) to get an idea of how powerful expected utility theory would become if it were valid for all situations.

ings of financial markets. The remainder of the chapter is organized as follows. We first describe a typical asset-pricing experiment. We then determine what the theory predicts about the outcomes in that experiment. Next, we discuss the actual outcomes in a series of experiments that were conducted at Caltech. We point out evidence showing that it is difficult to control subjects' assessment of uncertainty. That this happens even in a tightly controlled experimental setting raises some questions about beliefs in field markets (we address such questions in Chapter 6). Subsequently, we elaborate on the minimum scale (number of subjects) that is needed to observe full equilibration. Finally, we translate the evidence into statistical language, and ask what the chances are that we observe the outcomes we did if subjects were merely good speculators, and hence, prices were a random walk. That is, we formally test asset-pricing theory against the null of a random walk. Formal tests put the inference from experiments at the level of rigor that we expect in empirical analysis of historical data.

4.2 A Typical Asset-Pricing Experiment

Imagine the following situation. A number of subjects are endowed with a set of securities whose liquidation values depend on the realization of a state that is randomly drawn with commonly known probabilities (usually equal likelihood). The subjects are allowed to trade the securities during a certain period before the state is drawn and liquidation values are determined. They are also given some cash, because the securities are to be traded in markets where settlement occurs in terms of currency, to be called francs (F). After liquidation, values are determined and subjects are paid based on their final holdings of securities and cash minus a preset minimum threshold, to be thought of as the payment for the loan of securities.

Let there be three securities, two that are risky (Table 4.1 A and B), and one that is riskfree (Table 4.1 Notes). Their payoffs are determined by a matrix like the one displayed in Table 4.1. Securities A and B cannot be sold short, but the Notes can, up to a certain level (say, eight).

Trade takes place in web-based electronic open-book markets for each security. Subjects submit limit orders, which are either crossed

Table 4.1

Typical Payoff Matrix

Security	State		
	X	Y	Z
A	170	370	150
B	160	190	250
Notes	100	100	100

against opposing orders (at the price of the latter), or displayed in a book. The market setup is very much like those in the Paris Bourse or the Tel Aviv Stock Exchange. Subjects have access to the entire book. Identities are not revealed (each subject is assigned an individual ID number, which is the only identification that ever appears in the public records). Subjects have also access to the entire history of transactions, graphically and numerically. The trading interface is referred to as *Marketscape*.

The main web page of Marketscape is reproduced in Fig. 4.1. For each market, this core web page displays (1) individual holdings, (2) best standing bid and ask, (3) last transaction price, (4) personal best bid and ask, (5) access to historical data (individual and public), and (6) an order form. Inspection of the latter reveals that subjects can submit limit orders for multiple units, and can attach a deadline. The core web page has links to many other web pages, including instructions, help, and payout (i.e., dividend) history. Announcements are displayed on the main web page and logged in an announcements web page.

At the beginning of each trading period, subjects are endowed with a certain number of each security. Significantly, these endowments are private information only: the aggregate endowment is thus not known. As a matter of fact, since the trading is web-based, and therefore, physically decentralized subjects can form only a rough idea of the number of participants by looking at the open book, or the history of transactions.[25]

25. There is potential for collusion among subjects. In particular, two subjects may agree to the following strategy. Subject 1 offers to sell his inventory of risky securities at very low prices. Subject 2 buys it at those prices. Subject 1 will default and have to leave the experiment. Subject 2, however, will make plenty of money. Subjects 1 and 2 split the profits.

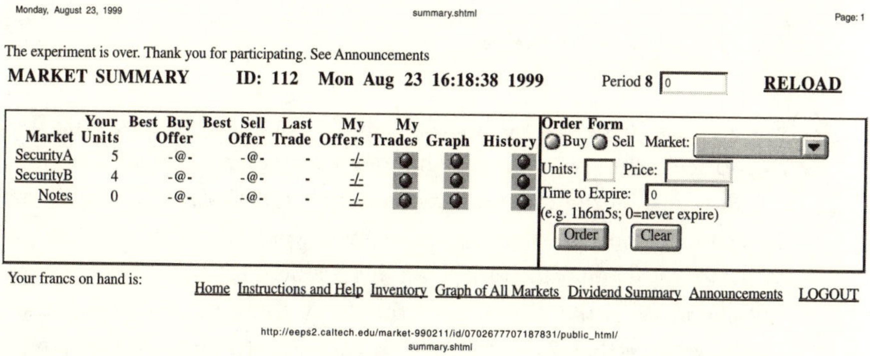

The experiment is over. Thank you for participating. See Announcements

MARKET SUMMARY   **ID: 112**   **Mon Aug 23 16:18:38 1999**   Period 8 [0   ]   **RELOAD**

Market	Your Units	Best Buy Offer	Best Sell Offer	Last Trade	My Offers	My Trades	Graph	History	Order Form
SecurityA	5	-@-	-@-	-	-/-	⊙	⊙	⊙	◯ Buy ◯ Sell Market: [▾]
SecurityB	4	-@-	-@-	-	-/-	⊙	⊙	⊙	Units: [ ] Price: [ ]
Notes	0	-@-	-@-	-	-/-	⊙	⊙	⊙	Time to Expire: [0]
									(e.g. 1h6m5s; 0=never expire)
									[Order] [Clear]

Your francs on hand is:

Home   Instructions and Help   Inventory   Graph of All Markets   Dividend Summary   Announcements   LOGOUT

http://eeps2.caltech.edu/market-990211/id/0702677707187831/public_html/
summary.shtml

Figure 4.1

Caltech's Marketscape Trading Interface.

No one is given privileged information about the likelihood of the states that are to be drawn at the end of each period. In other words, information is symmetric.

The endowment of cash is typically F400. Subjects cannot submit bids if they have insufficient cash to execute them. Thus there is a cash-in-advance constraint that will noticeably affect the interest rate in the experiments. A typical loan repayment is F1900. This amounts to a relatively · high level of leverage,[26] which is meant to amplify risk. The franc earnings are exchanged for U.S. dollars at a pre-announced exchange rate (e.g., $0.02 per franc).

Typically, an experiment runs for three or four hours, with periods of twenty-five minutes of trading, and five minutes break (to determine payouts, and to refresh the allocations of securities and cash). Subjects take home their cumulative earnings. If a subject has negative cumulative earnings for more than two periods, he or she is barred from further participation. The subjects are sometimes given a signup reward, so that they start out from a positive earnings position.

But random delay in relaying of orders and ability of others to snap up the advantageous sell offers make it impossible to implement this strategy successfully. Attempts are occasionally observed, but subjects stop as soon as they realize that it is impossible for two subjects to successfully target trades to each other.

26. With an initial allocation of 5 of A and 4 of B, and the payoff matrix in Table 4.1, the expected payment per period is only F450 ($= 400 + 5 \times 230 + 4 \times 200 - 1900$).

4.3   Theoretical Predictions

For a typical experiment described in the previous section, what does asset-pricing theory predict will happen to prices?

We consider the standard answer: for each period, the financial markets should equilibrate to the point that expected returns are proportional to aggregate risk. Translating this prediction into two specific asset-pricing models, the CAPM and the Arrow-Debreu complete-markets model (notice that the number of securities with independent payoffs equals the number of states, so that markets are indeed complete), this means:

1. Expected excess returns are proportional to market beta, or equivalently, the market portfolio is mean-variance optimal.
2. The ranking of the state prices should be the inverse of the ranking of the aggregate payout across the states.

The CAPM is more restrictive, as it assumes quadratic utility. But its prediction is more specific than that of the Arrow-Debreu model. Hopefully, a quadratic function approximates subjects' risk attitudes well enough for mean-variance analysis to obtain. Theoretically, the CAPM is indeed appropriate if risk is small; see Judd and Guu (2000). The experimental results confirm the theoretical prediction.

One aspect of these predictions deserves emphasis. It is possible to characterize equilibrium without knowing subjects' attitudes toward risk. They have only to be characterized as risk averse. No matter what the level of risk aversion is, the distance from equilibrium can be measured by how far the market portfolio is from mean-variance optimality (in the CAPM) or whether the ranking of state prices is inverse to the ranking of aggregate wealth (in the Arrow-Debreu model).

This is important, not only because experimenters do not know subjects' risk attitudes, but also because these attitudes may change through inevitable wealth changes in the trading that takes place before equilibrium is reached. The prices that support (instantaneous) equilibrium at the original endowments may no longer be valid after a few off-equilibrium trades. Still, the prices that support equilibrium at the new wealth levels must be such that the market portfolio is mean-variance optimal (in the CAPM) or they must imply state prices that are ranked inversely to aggregate payout (in the Arrow-Debreu model).

To test the CAPM, let us directly verify whether the market portfolio is mean-variance optimal. That is, let us measure the distance between the reward-to-risk ratio of the market portfolio ς_M and the maximum possible reward-to-risk ratio $\overline{\varsigma}$. These ratios are referred to as *Sharpe ratios*:

$$\varsigma_M = \frac{E[R_M - R_F]}{\sqrt{\text{var}(R_M - R_F)}}, \qquad [4.1]$$

$$\overline{\varsigma} = \max \frac{E[R_p - R_F]}{\sqrt{\text{var}(R_p - R_F)}}, \qquad [4.2]$$

where the maximum is to be taken over all possible portfolios of risky and riskfree securities, with typical return R_p. (In the experiments, states are drawn independently over time. Hence, we need not condition on a state vector x.)

The CAPM holds if:

$$\varsigma_M = \overline{\varsigma}.$$

One measure of the distance of the market from CAPM equilibrium is simply the absolute difference Δ_M:

$$\Delta_M = |\varsigma_M - \overline{\varsigma}|. \qquad [4.3]$$

Let us turn to the experimental results.

4.4 Experimental Results

In the Fall of 1998 and Spring of 1999, four experimental financial markets were organized as described earlier in this chapter.[27] The subjects came from the MBA population at the Yale School of Management, UCLA's Anderson Graduate School of Management, and Stanford's Graduate School of Business. Except in the experiments involving Yale students, Caltech students also participated. All subjects were familiar with financial markets through coursework.

---

27. More experiments have since been run. The interested reader should consult Bossaerts and Plott (1999), where the entire set is described in more detail.

Table 4.2

List of Experiments and Their Parameters

	Experiment						
		UCLA		Yale2		Stanford	
	Yale I	Group I	Group II	Group I	Group II	Group I	Group II
Number of subjects	30	23	21	8	11	22	22
Signup reward (F)	0	0	0	0	0	175	175
Allocation							
A	4	5	2	5	2	9	1
B	4	4	7	4	7	1	9
Notes	0	0	0	0	0	0	0
Cash (F)	400	400	400	400	400	400	400
Loan (F)	1900	2000	2000	2000	2000	2500	2400
Exchange rate ($/F)	0.03	0.03	0.03	0.03	0.03	0.04	0.04

Specifics of the experiments are provided in Table 4.2. Experiments are named after the affiliation of the majority of the subjects. Further details can be found in Bossaerts and Plott (1999). Here we give only the main results.

Figure 4.2 plots the evolution of the transaction prices of the three securities in the "Yale1" experiment. Each point corresponds to a transaction in one of the securities (the prices of the other securities are taken from their respective last transactions). We observe the following from the figure:

- Prices of risky securities generally lie below their expected payoffs, which is clear proof of risk aversion. If expected utility theory were all-encompassing, the evidence of risk aversion in the experiments would contradict the willingness of subjects to take on far greater risks in the field. Consequently, the experiments reject the assumption that a single expected utility function can be used to explain in a coherent way all choices that a subject ever makes in his/her life. At the same time, the presence of risk aversion in the laboratory provides an opportunity to test asset-pricing theory experimentally, for risk aversion is the basis of all asset-pricing theory.

- It is not clear whether the values in Fig. 4.2 are equilibrium prices. At first, one would doubt this, because there is a trend in the prices.
- The price of the Notes invariably starts below the payout of F100, implying a positive interest rate, only to increase to F100 by the end of each period. Because there is no time value to money (cash earns zero interest, and the time horizon is small), the equilibrium interest rate is zero. At the end of each period, the pricing of the Notes does reflect a zero interest rate. Early in the experiment, however, the positive interest rate suggests a binding cash-in-advance constraint: subjects borrow money to purchase one type of risky security without having to first procure the necessary cash by selling the other type. Cash-in-advance constraints have been used in macroeconomics to explain the role of money and riskfree bonds (see, e.g., Clower [1967] and Lucas [1982]), but have usually been associated with the purchase of goods, and not with portfolio rebalancing. It is the latter that drives the interest rate in the experiments.

The evolution of the prices in the other experiments is very similar, so we won't go into details. Instead, we ask whether the price evolution implies equilibration. This is not clear, from Fig. 4.2, because prices clearly trend. We will first use the CAPM to determine the distance from equilibrium. We then appeal to the Arrow-Debreu asset-pricing model.

Figure 4.3 plots the distance from CAPM equilibrium for each transaction. The distance is measured as Δ_M, that is, the difference between the Sharpe ratio of the market portfolio and the maximum Sharpe ratio (see (4.3)). Although it does take a substantial amount of time, the markets in "Yale1" eventually reach the CAPM equilibrium. This is solid support in favor of the CAPM, and contrasts with the empirical evidence from historical data, which we summarized in Chapter 3. It implies that CAPM is not merely a nice mathematical model, but that it also predicts the eventual pricing of risky securities in experimental financial markets. In other words, it has scientific value.

Figure 4.4 plots the evolution of the Arrow-Debreu securities (AD securities) prices implied by the transaction prices of securities A, B and the Notes. The AD securities prices were normalized to add up to

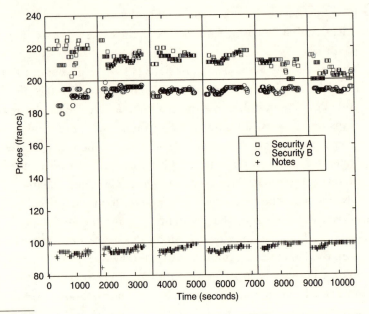

Figure 4.2

Transaction prices in experiment Yale1. Vertical lines delineate periods; horizontal lines show expected payoffs.

one. The resulting prices are known in mathematical finance as *state-price probabilities* or *equivalent martingale probabilities*. The Arrow-Debreu model predicts that the state prices, and hence, the state-price probabilities, will rank inversely to the aggregate payout (in this case, the payout on the market portfolio) across states. From Tables 4.1 and 4.2, it follows that the aggregate payout is highest in state Y, followed by state Z and X. Consequently, the state-price probability for state X should be highest, and that for state Y lowest.

Figure 4.4 shows that the prediction from the Arrow-Debreu model eventually obtains. In fact, early in the experiment, the state-price probability for X tends to increase, and that for Y tends to decrease, whereas that for Z attempts to position itself in the middle.

Again, this support for asset-pricing theory is not a consequence of subjects' pricing the AD securities deliberately in accordance with the theory, because subjects did not know the distribution of the aggregate payout across states. In fact, it is doubtful whether subjects cared about

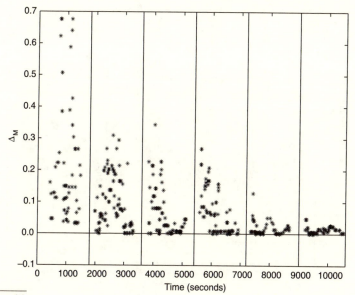

Figure 4.3

Distance from CAPM equilibrium (Δ_M) in experiment Yale1. Vertical lines
delineate periods.

AD securities at all. These were not directly traded. They could not even
have been created artificially as a portfolio of A, B, and the Notes, because
that would require one to shortsell at least one of the risky securities,
which was not allowed. And only a minority of subjects were familiar with
the notion of a state security, or state-price probabilities.

Let us turn to the evidence from one of the other experiments,
namely, UCLA. Figure 4.5 plots the evolution of the distance from CAPM
equilibrium, Δ_M. The evidence in support of the CAPM is even more
convincing than for the experiment Yale1. In particular, convergence is
much faster, perhaps because more subjects participated (see Table 4.2).

Figure 4.6 plots the evolution of the state-price probabilities in the
experiment UCLA. The ranking is in accordance with Arrow-Debreu
theory already from the second period on.

Altogether, such asset-pricing theory models as the CAPM and
the Arrow-Debreu model appear to predict quite well what eventually
emerges in experimental financial markets. The laboratory evidence

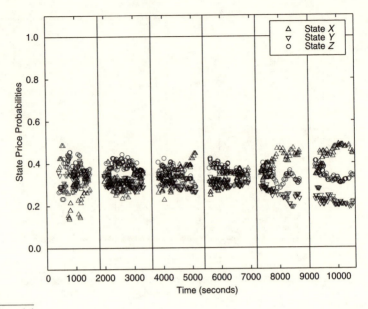

Figure 4.4

State-price probabilities (normalized AD securities prices), experiment Yale1. Vertical lines delineate periods.

supports the notion that markets equilibrate to the point that only co-variance with aggregate risk is priced.

But the experimental results also show that equilibration is far from instantaneous. Instead, it is a protracted process, lasting for several hours, even with only three securities. This finding calls for further theoretical analysis of price discovery in financial markets, perhaps along the lines of the tatonnement analysis suggested in Chapter 1. In addition, there is evidence that once equilibrium is reached, markets may move away from it, thereby defying the notion of equilibrium. Why is this? As we will discuss next, some of the movements can be explained by speculation.

4.5　Announced and Perceived Uncertainty

Let us focus on Fig. 4.5 and examine the deviation from equilibrium starting in period five and ending at the end of period six. For some

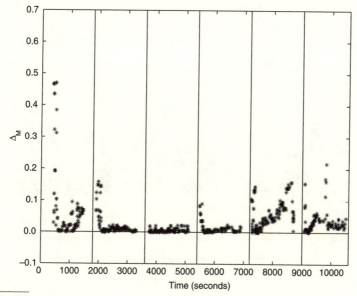

Figure 4.5

Distance from CAPM equilibrium (Δ_M) in experiment UCLA. Vertical lines delineate periods.

reason, markets in the UCLA experiment suddenly moved away from equilibrium and returned to it only slowly. Analysis of the state-price probabilities reveals that speculation may have been the cause. The state-price probabilities are shown in Fig. 4.6. An anomaly appears in period five as well, and extends nearly to the end of period six. In particular, state Z becomes cheaper. Its state-price probability falls below that of state Y, but the theory predicts that Z should be more expensive than Y.

What happened? A plausible explanation emerges when considering the sequence of states that was drawn in this experiment. From periods one to six, the states were, in order: Y, X, Z, Z, Y, X. By period five, state Z had occurred twice. Subjects may have read this as indicating that state Z was less likely to occur. Of course, this inference was wrong, as the drawing of states was independent over time, as if drawing one of three colored balls from an urn, with replacement. Because subjects may have lowered their assessments of the likelihood of state Z, they implicitly bid down the AD securities price of state Z.

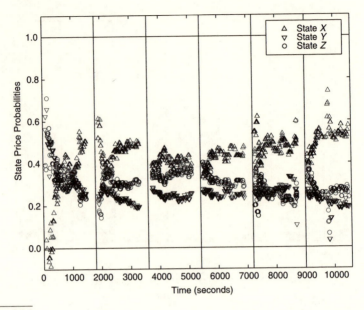

Figure 4.6

State-price probabilities (normalized AD securities prices), experiment UCLA. Vertical lines delineate periods.

This explanation is based on the subjects' confusion about the nature of randomness in the experiment. Even if they were told that the drawing is random with replacement (or could so infer from the occurrence of states in the trial period preceding the actual experiment), they may not have understood the consequences of the drawing. Instead, their vision of uncertainty may have been that of random drawing from an urn without replacement. Equivalently, subjects confuse "equal likelihood" with "equal frequency": when the experimenter announces that each of three states will be drawn with equal likelihood, they interpret this as meaning that each state will occur approximately the same number of times in the experiment.

We would not pay so much attention to the anomaly in UCLA, were it not that it became amplified in the Stanford experiment. It is far more apparent in this experiment that confusion about randomness can explain the results.

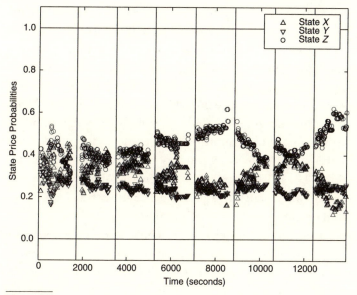

Figure 4.7

State-price probabilities (normalized AD securities prices), experiment Stanford. Vertical lines delineate periods.

Consider first the state-price probabilities in the Stanford experiment (see Fig. 4.7). Experimental results agree with theory by the end of the first and second period, but from the third period on, the price of state Z increases gradually, far beyond the price of state X, despite a much lower aggregate payout (see Table 4.2). In period six, the price of state Z crashes abruptly, so that, by the end of that period, state-price probabilities are again in line with the Arrow-Debreu theory. In periods seven and eight, the price of state Z again climbs to abnormally high levels relative to the theory.

As before, the particular sequence of states that was drawn in the Stanford experiment provides a plausible explanation. Across periods, the states were in order: X, Y, Y, X, Z, Y, X, Y. By the fourth period, some subjects had become convinced that period Z had to be next, because it had not yet been drawn (of course, this is nonsense), and hence, they implicitly bid up the price of state Z. When state X actually occurred, they apparently became even more convinced that Z had to be next (they happened to be right!), making matters worse. In period seven, the same speculation re-emerged. Because Z had only occurred once, some subjects were convinced it had to be drawn next, interpreting incorrectly that equal likelihood means equal frequency, or that states were drawn without replacement. Again, they implicitly bid up the price of state Z.

The anomaly in the state-price probabilities translated into problems for the CAPM. The top graph in Fig. 4.8 displays the evolution of the distance of the markets in Stanford experiment from the CAPM equilibrium. Convergence obtains in periods one and two, but starts to fail by period three. The markets revert back to the CAPM equilibrium only in period seven (when state-price probabilities also revert back to the Arrow-Debreu equilibrium), and briefly in period eight.

One can assess the plausibility of our conjecture that a confusion between drawing with and without replacement caused the anomaly, by recomputing the distance from CAPM equilibrium, Δ_M, based on the following model of uncertainty. Let subjects conjecture (incorrectly) that states are drawn without replacement from an urn with four balls of type X, four of type Y, and four of type Z. The total number of balls (twelve) is arbitrary, but provides a good starting point.

Under this belief structure, states that occurred less frequently will be assigned higher chances of occurring next. For instance, state Z would have 50 percent chance after the fourth round, whereas states X and Y would occur only with 25 percent probability, having both been drawn twice before. These probabilities are based on the hypergeometric distribution. Hence, we should refer to the resulting beliefs as *hypergeometric beliefs*.

One can easily recompute the maximum Sharpe ratio and the Sharpe ratio for hypergeometric beliefs. The bottom panel of Fig. 4.8 plots the resulting measure of the distance from CAPM equilibrium, Δ_M. The hypergeometric belief structure gives the CAPM a remarkably good fit all the way up to and including period six, after which its performance declines rapidly. The evidence suggests that markets equilibrated even in periods four, five and six, although based on a wrong perception of how states were drawn.

This evidence in favor of hypergeometric beliefs suggests that it may be worthwhile to organize future experiments around random draws with replacement instead of the usual draws without replacement. The experi-

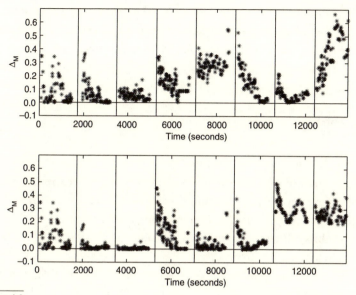

Figure 4.8

Distance from CAPM equilibrium (Δ_M) in experiment Stanford. Top panel, based on announced likelihood of states. Bottom panel, based on falsely interpreting the drawing of states as taking place without replacement. Vertical lines delineate periods.

menter should accommodate subjects' natural inclinations because asset-pricing theory does not prescribe how subjects should perceive risk, but instead, how risk perceptions lead to equilibration at the market level. In other words, the experimental evidence calls for better control of subjects' beliefs. Notice that this is a design issue, not a weakness of the theory, because the theory is silent about what beliefs subjects hold (although the model does assume that all subjects hold the same beliefs).

It is surprising how hard it is to model subjects' beliefs even in such simple experiments as the Stanford. One wonders whether beliefs are also ill-founded in naturally occurring financial markets. If they are, it is inappropriate to build an empirical methodology of tests of asset-pricing models entirely on the extreme assumption of correct priors. As explained in Chapter 2, correct priors constitute one of the two pillars of the efficient markets hypothesis (EMH).

If priors are regularly incorrect, then EMH cannot be appealed to in empirical methodology. Instead, a different set of tests must be designed that allows at least part of the prior to be biased and even erratic. This will be the topic of Chapter 5.

4.6   The Scale of Experimentation

Among the four experiments listed in Table 4.2, Yale2 involved far fewer subjects (nineteen) than the others (thirty or more). Experiments that were run earlier at Caltech within the same framework but with far fewer subjects (a maximum of 13), demonstrate that the resulting market thinness inhibits full equilibration (see Bossaerts and Plott [2001]). The experience in Yale2 confirms this.

Figure 4.9 plots the evolution of the distance from CAPM equilibrium in the experiment Yale2. Convergence is slow, and markets fail to

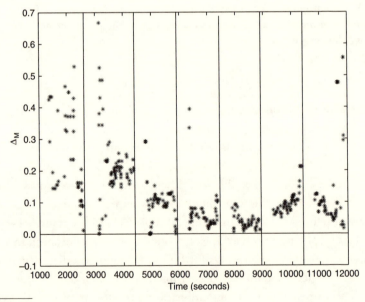

Figure 4.9

Distance from CAPM equilibrium (Δ_M) in experiment Yale2. Vertical lines delineate periods.

fully reach the CAPM. Also, state-price probabilities never convincingly reached the point where the Arrow-Debreu theory is supported (see Fig. 4.10).

This finding demonstrates that markets have to be sufficiently liquid for the predictions of asset-pricing theory to emerge. In a certain sense, it is not surprising. Asset-pricing theory is based on the competitive paradigm, where individuals cannot affect the prices at which they trade. When there are too few subjects, the terms of exchange can be influenced by such strategic tricks as delaying offers and trades.

Liquidity also provides subjects with the opportunity to rebalance quickly a portfolio in markets that do not allow them to submit limit orders conditional on events in another market. It is possible that the ability to readily rebalance entire portfolios is important for the empirical relevance of asset-pricing theory. Wohl and Kandel (1997) demonstrate theoretically how price discovery is enhanced when agents are allowed to submit orders that are conditioned on information across all markets.

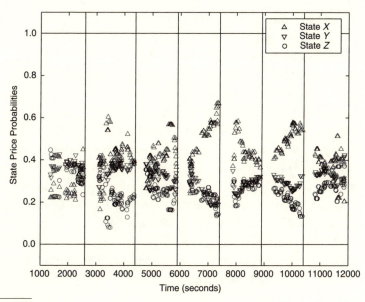

Figure 4.10

State-price probabilities (normalized AD securities prices), experiment Yale2. Vertical lines delineate periods.

Experimental financial markets in which trade is organized using a portfolio trading mechanism confirm this conjecture (see Bossaerts, Fine, and Ledyard [2000]).

4.7   Formal Tests

So far, we have produced graphical evidence of how well asset-pricing theory explains pricing in experimental financial markets. The graphical evidence should be complemented with formal tests, because it may be misleading. It has long been recognized in the analysis of historical data that graphical evidence cannot be taken at face value, but has to be confirmed by formal econometrics. For instance, we documented in Chapter 3 that it is of no consequence that Rubinstein's model plots below the Hansen-Jagannathan bound; sampling error had to be taken into account. Once that was done, the distance turned out to be insignificant (see the discussion on page 88).

We introduce a statistical test that formally distinguishes two hypotheses: (1) prices are unpredictable, that is they form a random walk (the null hypothesis), and (2) prices are driven by the economic forces predicted by asset-pricing theory, that is they are attracted, albeit stochastically, by equilibrium (the alternative hypothesis). The test effectively asks: what are the chances that we read too much (by positing asset-pricing theory) in the data, when in fact there is nothing going on besides speculation? Speculation will eliminate arbitrage opportunities, and, if subjects are risk neutral, causes prices to behave like random walks. Even if prices are a random walk, with only three securities, it is likely that the market portfolio accidentally becomes mean-variance efficient, confirming the CAPM, or that state-price probabilities happen to rank in accordance with Arrow-Debreu equilibrium. We want to rule out the possibility that our observations are cases of mere luck.

Let us first consider formal tests of the CAPM. Subsequently, we investigate the Arrow-Debreu model.

4.7.1   The CAPM

We take the random walk hypothesis as the null, and test it against the hypothesis that the market is pulled toward the CAPM. Our test works as follows. As before, let $\Delta_{M,t}$ denote the distance between the Sharpe ratio of the market and the maximum Sharpe ratio. We add the subscript t, to denote transaction time. Consider the projection of the change in $\Delta_{M,t}$ onto $\Delta_{M,t-1}$:

$$\Delta_{M,t} - \Delta_{M,t-1} = \kappa \, \Delta_{M,t-1} + \epsilon_t, \qquad [4.4]$$

where κ is such that ϵ_t is uncorrelated with $\Delta_{M,t-1}$. CAPM implies $\Delta_{M,t} = 0$; convergence to CAPM pricing implies $\kappa < 0$. We then determine the distribution of the least squares estimates of κ under the null hypothesis of a random walk, by randomly drawing from (i.e., bootstrapping) the empirical joint distribution of changes in transaction prices. The null hypothesis of a random walk is rejected in favor of stochastic convergence to CAPM if the least squares estimate of κ is beyond a critical value in the left tail of the resultant distribution. This testing procedure is a variation of *indirect inference* (see Gouriéroux, Monfort, and Renault [1993]): we summarize the data in terms of a simple statistical model (in our case, a least squares projection) and determine the distribution of the estimates by simulating the variables entering the statistical model. Instead of simulating from a theoretical distribution, we bootstrap the empirical distribution.[28]

For each experiment, we estimated κ using ordinary least squares. Five percent and 10 percent critical values under the random walk null hypothesis were determined by bootstrapping from the empirical joint distribution of price changes (we generated two hundred price series of the same length as the sample used to estimate κ).[29]

Table 4.3 reports the results. The null of a random walk is rejected in all experiments, including Yale2. The statistical analysis indicates that there is only a tiny probability to obtain accidentally, for instance, the plot in Fig. 4.9, if prices indeed form a random walk.

The rejections of the random-walk hypothesis reported in Table 4.3 do not imply that the subjects ignored profit opportunities from speculating on price changes. This is because our rejection of the random walk is based on information that subjects could not condition on, namely, the

28. Gallant and Tauchen (1996) also use indirect inference, but, instead of matching an arbitrary statistical model, they match the scores of the likelihood function.

29. We bootstrapped the mean-corrected empirical distribution, to stay within the null hypothesis of a random walk.

Table 4.3

Test of Random-Walk Pricing Against Stochastic Attraction Toward CAPM Equilibrium

| Experiment | Estimate[1] | Attraction Coefficient κ | |
| | | Critical Value[2] | |
		5 percent	10 percent
Yale1	-0.103^*	-0.013	-0.009
UCLA	-0.081^*	-0.009	-0.004
Yale2	-0.462^*	-0.219	-0.081
Stanford	-0.016^*	-0.009	-0.006

[1]Meaning of superscripts: * = significant at the 5 percent level.

[2]Based on two hundred bootstrapped samples of the same size as used to estimate κ.

Sharpe ratio of the market portfolio. This ratio is not readily determined from the history of price movements: its computation requires knowledge of the composition of the market portfolio. As emphasized before, subjects did not know this, and hence, could not determine in which way prices would move when the market was still out of equilibrium, even if they believed in the CAPM.

4.7.2 The Arrow-Debreu Model

The graphical evidence strongly suggests that state-price probabilities moved in the direction predicted by Arrow-Debreu equilibrium, even if their ranking contradicted the theory for long periods of time. We need a formal test to confirm the visual evidence of movement. In particular, we want to determine whether state price probabilities adjust toward Arrow-Debreu equilibrium when their ranking is not as predicted by the theory. We again take random-walk pricing as our null hypothesis. That is, we determine what the probability is of observing the dynamics in state-price probabilities in our experiments if prices were merely random walks (i.e., unpredictable, and hence, unaffected by economic forces beyond the absence of speculative profit opportunities). Under the alternative that markets are attracted by Arrow-Debreu equilibrium, we expect specific changes in the state-price probabilities when they are not aligned appropriately. In particular, we expect the results shown in Table 4.4.

Table 4.4

Ranking of State-Price Probabilities at a Moment in Time and Expected Effect on Subsequent Changes in State-Price Probabilities

Ranking of State-Price Probabilities at t^1	Expected Effect
$P_{X,t} > P_{Y,t} > P_{Z,t}$	$(P_{Z,t+1} - P_{Y,t+1}) - (P_{Z,t} - P_{Y,t}) > 0$
$P_{X,t} > P_{Z,t} > P_{Y,t}$	Anything is Possible
$P_{Y,t} > P_{X,t} > P_{Z,t}$	$(P_{X,t+1} - P_{Y,t+1}) - (P_{X,t} - P_{Y,t}) > 0$
$P_{Y,t} > P_{Z,t} > P_{X,t}$	$(P_{X,t+1} - P_{Y,t+1}) - (P_{X,t} - P_{Y,t}) > 0$
	or $(P_{Z,t+1} - P_{Y,t+1}) - (P_{Z,t} - P_{Y,t}) > 0$
$P_{Z,t} > P_{Y,t} > P_{X,t}$	$(P_{X,t+1} - P_{Y,t+1}) - (P_{X,t} - P_{Y,t}) > 0$
$P_{Z,t} > P_{X,t} > P_{Y,t}$	$(P_{X,t+1} - P_{Z,t+1}) - (P_{X,t} - P_{Z,t}) > 0$

$^1P_{X,t}$, $P_{Y,t}$ and $P_{Z,t}$ denote the time-t state-price probabilities for states X, Y and Z, respectively. Time is measured in number of transactions.

These predictions are weak, because they only concern the sign of the change in the difference between two state-price probabilities. The question is: are economic forces strong enough that the expected effects can be detected sharply?

As test statistic, we compute the frequency of transiting to the expected outcome for each state (i.e., ranking of state-price probabilities). We subsequently average across states. The averaging is mandated because in finite samples, not all states need occur, in which case some transition frequencies are undefined. Let π denote the mean transition frequency. Notice that the second frequency will always be 1 (100 percent). We include this frequency, so that outcomes where the Arrow Debreu prediction holds ($P_{X,t} > P_{Z,t} > P_{Y,t}$) receive more weight. In analogy with our formal test of the Sharpe ratio property, we compute the distribution of π under the null hypothesis by bootstrapping the empirical joint distribution of price changes in each experiment (we generated two hundred price series of the same length as the sample used to estimate π).[30]

Table 4.5 reports the results. In addition to the estimated mean transition frequencies (second column), we report 5 percent, 90 percent and 95 percent critical values under the null of random-walk pricing. The striking aspect of the estimated mean transition frequencies is not only that they are highly significant, but also that they are remarkably

30. We bootstrapped the mean-corrected empirical distribution, in order to stay with the null hypothesis of a random walk.

constant across experiments. There are pronounced differences across experiments in terms of beginning prices and empirical distribution of price changes, which translate into marked differences in the distribution of π under the null of a random- walk.[31] Across all experiments, the estimated values for π are almost always the same, however, suggesting that the same forces are at work. They are in the right tail of the distribution under the null, and are uniformly significant at the 5 percent level. Overall, Table 4.5 provides formal evidence that Arrow Debreu equilibrium predicts price movements in experimental financial markets better than the random-walk hypothesis.

As before, the rejections of the random-walk hypothesis reported in Table 4.5 do not imply that the subjects ignored profit opportunities from speculating on price changes. This is because our rejection of the random walk is based on information that subjects could not condition on, namely, the distribution of aggregate wealth across states.

4.8   Conclusion

More can be said about financial market experiments and additional results are available. For instance, the CAPM makes a strong prediction about allocations, namely, portfolio separation: all subjects should eventually hold the same portfolio of risky securities. See the discussion preceding (1.22) in Chapter 1. Bossaerts, Plott, and Zame (2000) examines portfolio separation in experimental financial markets. Also, price dynamics can be studied, for example, by means of the system of ordinary differential equations (1.45) in Chapter 1, which obtained in a competitive price discovery model. We do not discuss these topics here, partly because empirical analysis of historical data has focused on equilibrium pricing and ignored issues of allocations and price discovery.[32]

31. If the initial price configuration satisfies or is close to satisfying the Arrow Debreu equilibrium restriction, the simulated values for π will be high (the predicted outcome if $P_{X,t} > P_{Z,t} > P_{Y,t}$ obtains with unit frequency). This explains the high level of the 5 percent critical value for the Stanford experiment. Thus our procedure penalizes experiments that happen to start out with prices that closely or exactly satisfy Arrow Debreu equilibrium restrictions.

32. There has been a change in this focus recently. For instance, Heaton and Lucas (2000) studies allocations.

Table 4.5

Test of Random-Walk Pricing Against Stochastic Attraction Toward Arrow-Debreu Equilibrium

| | | Mean Transition Probability π | | |
| | | | Critical Value[2] | |
Experiment	Estimate[1]	5 percent	90 percent	95 percent
Yale1	0.88*	0.31	0.61	0.59
UCLA	0.87*	0.25	0.48	0.51
Yale2	0.84*	0.39	0.79	0.83
Stanford	0.89*	0.64	0.83	0.85

[1]Meaning of superscripts: * = significant at the 95 percent level.

[2]Based on two hundred bootstrapped samples of the same size as used to estimate π.

As far as asset pricing is concerned, this chapter documented that the evidence from experimental financial markets is overall favorable. This should give us renewed interest in understanding why empirical research on historical data has failed. At the end of the previous chapter, we conjectured that the assumption of correct beliefs (one of the pillars of EMH) may be responsible. The experimental results underscore the fragility of beliefs, even in a laboratory environment. Consequently, the time is ripe to consider changes to the empirical methodology that allow for biases in the market's beliefs, even if only partial.

CHAPTER 5

From EMH to Merely Efficient Learning

5.1 Introduction

In Chapter 1, we derived the main prediction of asset-pricing theory: the market will set prices such that it expects excess returns on risky securities to be proportional to their covariance with aggregate risk. In Chapter 2, we saw how traditional empirical tests verify this theoretical prediction by comparing ex-post sample average excess returns and sample covariances. (The averages and covariances may be conditional.) The strategy implicitly assumes that (1) the market's ex ante expectations are correct, and (2) returns and aggregate risk are stationary. Together, these two assumptions are referred to as the efficient markets hypothesis (EMH). In Chapter 3, we summarized the empirical evidence from studies of historical field data. We generally found little support for asset-pricing theory. The complexity of historical analysis makes it hard to determine the reasons for the rejections. Still, lack of stationarity did not appear to be the cause. In Chapter 4, we reported experimental evidence that showed that the basic principles of the theory do explain pricing in simple laboratory markets. But we noticed two phenomena: (1) the theory predicts properties of pricing in equilibrium, yet markets take some time to equilibrate; (2) even with a select group of subjects, it is hard to account for the beliefs of the market.

If we take the experimental evidence at face value, then there are two potentially fruitful routes that we can explore to explain the empirical failures on historical field data. One is the possibility that financial markets are most often not in equilibrium, but on a path toward equilibrium. The other is to explore empirical restrictions that obtain even if we relax the assumption that the market must hold correct beliefs.

Little work has been done on the first route.[33] In contrast, the second route has been explored in more depth over the last few years, and has so far produced promising results. So let us focus on the second route, and leave the first route for future work. In this chapter, we describe how we are going to relax EMH and still obtain robust empirical restrictions that rely on as little information as possible about the historical environment from which the data are extracted.

We do not need experiments to justify relaxing the assumption of correct beliefs. While correctness of beliefs may eventually describe the outcome of a long learning process in a stationary world, it is not clear that the world is stationary, or whether the beginning of our historical datasets always coincides with the end of the learning process. Hence, it seems impossible to ignore learning.[34] To hedge against the possibility that markets have not learned everything yet, it pays to develop a testing strategy that is immune to learning effects.

We want the testing strategy to use information as parsimoniously as that based on EMH. We do not want to add parameters. Among other things, this means that we do not want to estimate the biases in market beliefs at a particular point in time. Instead, we want to focus on change, and derive properties of returns that obtain no matter what the beliefs were before the change took place.

Such a testing strategy will inevitably approach historical data differently than previous tests have done. It will no longer be possible to ask whether average returns over a period of history are in line with theo-

33. As mentioned before, however, there is theoretical and empirical work on market microstructure models. These models can be considered as equilibrium discovery models. But the link with asset-pricing theory is not made explicit. Moreover, market microstructure models are game-theoretic, and hence, are equilibrium models themselves, which just pushes the issue one level back: how do markets discover the equilibria of the microstructure models?

34. Bossaerts (1995) proves that econometric tests of asset-pricing theory cannot ignore transient learning, even if based on asymptotics.

retical predictions. Instead, we will have to focus on change. How does a market move from one price level to another? Are the price changes (i.e., returns) consistent with rational reaction to information by a risk-averse market? The focus is on transition rather than long-run averages.

Our tests require the empiricist to think about historical datasets as *cross-sections*. That is not a problem with datasets that come naturally as cross-sections, such as the U.S. initial public offering (IPO) aftermarket performance records we dealt with in Chapter 3. For other historical datasets, however, it means that the dataset must be rearranged. For instance, Bossaerts (1998) investigates the history of S&P 500 returns in the period 1928–97. This history comes naturally as a single time series. But it can be rearranged as a cross-section of overlapping histories, each with a length of, say, nine trading days.

We then investigate the price dynamics in each history of our cross-section. We let the market prior be arbitrary at the beginning of each history. That is, it need not be specified in what way the prior is wrong. It may even be right. The prior may also vary from one history to another. There can be a relationship between the outcome at the end of one history and the prior at the beginning of another history. This arises naturally when rearranging the time series of S&P 500 returns in the period 1928–97 as a cross-section of nine-day histories (see Bossaerts [1998]). But the relationship need not be specified.

The *market prior* is understood as the probability distribution reflected in equilibrium prices. That is, it is the probability distribution such that the expectations of excess returns are proportional to the corresponding covariances between excess returns and aggregate risk. There are fundamental questions about how this market prior relates to the beliefs of individual market participants. Of course, one could assume that all beliefs are essentially identical. (In fact, this assumption is common in game theory, where it is known as the Harsanyi doctrine— see Harsanyi [1967].) In general, there may be different beliefs, and it is not immediately clear how they aggregate (but see Biais and Bossaerts [1998].) An investigation of this issue would distract us, so let us not elaborate further.

The market prior concerns a security's payoff at some future point. In the case of the U.S. IPOs, it is the subjective probability distribution of the value of an IPO, say, five years after the IPO date. In Bossaerts (1998), the market's prior is the belief about the value of the S&P 500 index nine trading days later. (We can also take some other future reference point, of course.)

We require that the market use all available information to update its prior. The updating is Bayesian, as is standard in EMH. We generally will not specify what the information is. As before, we will merely refer to it as some state vector x. At some point, however, we will have to inquire whether we need to know all of x for our tests. This question had to be addressed in the context of standard tests of asset-pricing theory based on EMH. Some of the tests are immune to deletion of information, which means that the empiricist does not have to know much about the historical environment from which the data were taken (see Chapter 2).

In updating its beliefs, the market uses the likelihood function of future information, given past information, and given the final outcome (i.e., the payout). We will assume that this likelihood is correct, in the sense that it corresponds to the actual large-sample frequencies of future information given past information and the final outcome. This assumption is an integral part of standard EMH. But EMH also requires that the prior be correct, that is, that it coincide with the large-sample distribution of the final payout across histories. We drop this last requirement.

Summarizing, we hypothesize the following about market beliefs:

1. At the beginning of each history in the dataset, the market's prior is arbitrary. Moreover, the prior may change from one history to another.
2. During each history, the market's updating is Bayesian.
3. The updating is based on the correct likelihood of future information given past information and the final outcome.

Because we deviate from EMH only in the restriction on the prior, and leave the assumptions on learning intact, we refer to our set of hypotheses as those of an *efficiently learning market*, and use the acronym ELM.

To clarify its meaning, it may be useful to give a nonfinancial example of the equivalent of ELM. Imagine an individual who is dropped one day at some random point on earth where she has never been before. She is asked to predict whether it is going to rain the next day. Of course, because our individual is visiting the place for the first time, she may not be well informed about the unconditional probability that it will rain the next day. But her experience with rain elsewhere should allow her to update her prior correctly. She knows that rain is often preceded by a certain type of clouds. These clouds are far less likely when the next day is rainfree. That is, she knows the likelihood of the state of nature (in this case, type of clouds) given that it will rain the next day, or given that it will not rain the next day. With this information (state and likelihood) she updates her prior and announces her prediction. As for individuals in our financial market, the individual holds a potentially biased prior, determined by her own particular experience elsewhere. And like them, she does not ignore the available information that carries a signal about future events. She updates her prior using the correct likelihood function.

It may still sound implausible to assume that the likelihood function is correct. Our individual may not be good at reading the sky. Similarly, a market may be asked to predict the value of a biotech company five years in the future, when this company's only product is a novel medication with which scientists have no experience. Hence, they cannot even determine correctly what the probability of failure of a clinical trial would be even if the medication eventually turns out to be effective.

Our allowing the prior to be arbitrary is a major departure from EMH. It immediately brings up an interesting question: will we always be able to explain any price history in terms of a well-chosen prior? (Of course, we will assume specific attitudes toward risk, and hence, risk premiums.) If so, it is of little use to relax EMH further, because ELM is without empirical content. Fortunately, the answer is a firm no. That is, merely allowing the market's prior to be arbitrary does not enable one to explain away every pricing anomaly.

Because the market's prior can be arbitrary, tests of ELM in conjunction with an asset-pricing model focus on the correctness of updating: the usage of Bayes' law together with a correct likelihood function. Tests of ELM reveal whether the market sets prices correctly upon receiving new information. Does it overreact to information (which would imply excessive volatility) or does it underreact (volatility is too low)? Overreaction and underreaction should be measured relative to the market's own beliefs, and not relative to the correct belief.

In fact, what is the "correct belief," anyway? Historical datasets often come with incredibly subtle selection biases, so that the frequency distribution of recorded payouts does not necessarily provide a good estimate of the correct belief. Moreover, certain outcomes could reasonably have been expected but happened not to occur in the history at hand. In both cases, a comparison of the market prior with the recorded frequency of outcomes will reveal discrepancies, even if the former is correct.

Many researchers have recently raised the possibility of selection biases. See Brown, Goetzmann, and Ross (1995), Goetzmann and Jorion (1999), and Danthine and Donaldson (1999) for support of the view that selection biases cause the high equity premium that U.S. stock markets have historically enjoyed. One argument is, for instance, that one has to offset the phenomenal price runup in the U.S. markets in the 1990s with the dismal performance of the Japanese markets. The average of the two markets looks far more reasonable from an asset-pricing theoretic point of view.

One of the most attractive aspects of the methodology introduced in this chapter is that it does not make any reference to a "correct belief." It need not be estimated; it need not even be defined conceptually. This will be apparent when we establish that tests of ELM will work on biased samples. We will not need a record of all possible outcomes that the market or the empiricist expects. After all, we are not really studying average performance over long time series, but changes (i.e., price movements) in cross-sections of shorter histories.

In Chapter 6, our tests of ELM (together with a simple asset-pricing model) on U.S. IPO return data will be based only on the winners, that is, the IPOs that did not fail within a certain period of time. We will ignore losers. Throwing away the losers obviously biases a study of the average aftermarket performance of U.S. IPOs. But it will not bias a study of whether the market correctly updates prices of IPOs that will ultimately turn out to be winners, given beliefs and risk attitudes at the IPO date.[35]

It has already been mentioned that we do not need to specify the

---

35. Similarly, Bossaerts (1998) looked at the S&P 500 history, but discarded some events without affecting the inference. For instance, a 15 percent drop occurred on one day in the 1980s, but this event was not used. Of course, throwing away such an event in a study of the average performance of the S&P 500 over the past twenty years would seriously bias some results. But it does not bias a study of whether the S&P 500 correctly absorbs new information.

market prior. To get simple, robust tests of ELM, however, we cannot be completely arbitrary. We examine the pricing of such limited-liability securities as equity. There is a positive probability that these securities pay nothing, an event that is described generically as *default*. A number of restrictions obtain only if we allow the market's prior about default to be arbitrary, but leave the prior correct in other respects. In particular, the market may be wrong about the probability of default (i.e., probability that the security pays nothing), but, if the security does not default (i.e., if it pays a positive amount), then the market should have predicted correctly the expected payout. In other words, the market may not know the probability of default, but does know correctly the mean payout conditional on no default.

Other auxiliary assumptions may have to be made. For instance, we will invoke a *no early exclusion hypothesis* (NEEH), which, loosely speaking, states that the final outcome is never known with certainty until the end of the history being considered. Notice that we do not specify the prior. We are only providing a broad characterization.

Let us now turn to the mathematics. In the next section, we provide a few details about Bayesian updating, and prove a simple property that is the cornerstone of the empirical implications of ELM. Subsequently, we will discuss the pricing of relatively simple securities: digital options and, more generally, limited-liability securities. This will allow us to revisit an example from Chapter 2.

5.2 Bayesian Learning

Here is the canonical model of Bayesian learning. Let t index time: $t = 0, 1, \ldots, T$. A Bayesian learner is asked to predict the outcome of a parameter V, a real random variable, to be revealed at T. Initially, her prior belief about the distribution of V can be summarized by a density or probability mass function λ_0, which is a function of V.

The prior λ_0 is arbitrary. In particular, it need not coincide with the true probability from which V is drawn. In fact, the latter may be trivial, as when the Bayesian learner is asked to guess the distance between Pasadena and Toulouse; this is a random variable for our learner, but a fixed number for those who have measured it.

The arbitrariness of λ_0 is meant to map into the first building block of ELM, namely, that the market holds an unspecified prior belief about the final payoff of a security. The mapping becomes clear once the parameter V is interpreted as the final payoff.

At $t = 1, \ldots, T-1$, the Bayesian learner receives a number of signals, taken to be real numbers, and collected in a vector x_t. Conditional on the parameter V, the signal process is Markovian, which implies that the likelihood function (either a density or a probability mass function) of x_t given V and the history of $\{x_{t-1}, x_{t-2}, \ldots\}$ can be written solely in terms of x_{t-1} and V:

$$l_t(x_t | x_{t-1}, V).$$

The subscript t allows the likelihood to vary over time. When $t = 1$, there is no prior history, and we write:

$$l_1(x_1 | V).$$

We impose the restriction that the parameter V does not define the boundaries (i.e., the upper and lower limits, if they exist) of x_t. We need this restriction when interchanging integration over V and over x_t.

We assume that the Bayesian learner knows the likelihood function $l_t(x_t | x_{t-1}, V)$. This is restrictive, but is implicit in EMH as well. It is also tacitly assumed in standard Bayesian analysis. Our learner updates her beliefs on the basis of Bayes' law. If λ_t denotes her posterior belief over V, given $x_1, \ldots, x_t$, this means:

$$\lambda_t(V) = \frac{l_t(x_t | x_{t-1}, V)\lambda_{t-1}(V)}{\int l_t(x_t | x_{t-1}, v)\lambda_{t-1}(v)\,dv}, \quad (t = 1, 2, \ldots, T-1). \quad [5.1]$$

Bayesian updating is known to be rational, in the sense that the learner formulates her posterior belief in such a way that she cannot predict how her posterior belief will subsequently change. Mathematically, this property is known as *Doob's martingale result* (Doob [1948]):

$$E^m[\lambda_t(V) | x_{t-1}, \ldots, x_1] = \lambda_{t-1}(V). \quad [5.2]$$

The superscript m to the expectations operator conveys that expectations are taken with respect to the learner's own subjective beliefs, and not with respect to the true probability measure. That is:

$$E^m[\lambda_t(V) | x_{t-1}, ldots, x_1] = \int \int \lambda_t(V)l_t(x | x_{t-1}, v)\lambda_{t-1}(v)\,dx\,dv.$$

(This equation should make it easy to prove Doob's martingale result; see the Exercises.)

Because it obtains only with respect to the learner's subjective beliefs, Doob's martingale result is of limited interest empirically. There is a restriction, however, that does obtain under the true probability measure.

Of course, the notion of a true probability measure is ambiguous, as already pointed out. But we do agree on the objective nature of one density function, namely, the likelihood $l_t(x_t|x_{t-1}, V)$. So, let us explore expectations with respect to this density. That is, let us analyze expectations conditional on the final outcome V. These will be denoted as follows:

$$E[\cdot|x_{t-1}, V](= E[\cdot|x_{t-1}, \ldots, x_1, V]).$$

The Markov assumption justifies the equality in parentheses.

Now consider the conditional expectation of the ratio of the time $(t - 1)$ posterior and the time t posterior $(t = 1, \ldots, T - 1)$, both evaluated at a fixed V^*:

$$E\left[\frac{\lambda_{t-1}(V^*)}{\lambda_t(V^*)}|x_{t-1}, V\right].$$

We first have to ensure that this conditional expectation is well-defined. The standard definition requires that the unconditional expectation be finite:

$$E\left[\left|\frac{\lambda_{t-1}(V^*)}{\lambda_t(V^*)}\right|\right] < \infty. \qquad [5.3]$$

But we do not know what this unconditional expectation is, because it depends not only on the likelihood functions $l_\tau(x_\tau|x_{\tau-1}, V)$ $(\tau = 1, \ldots, t)$, but also on the true distribution of V, about which we chose to be noncommittal.

There is one way to ensure that (5.3) holds no matter what unconditional distribution we elect for V: we could bluntly assume that the posterior is always bounded away from zero. That is, there exists $\epsilon > 0$ such that, for all V^*, and for $t = 0, 1, \ldots, T - 1$:

$$P\{\lambda_t(V^*) \geq \epsilon|V\} = 1, \qquad [5.4]$$

where the probability P is computed from $l_1(x_1|V), \ldots, l_t(x_t|x_{t-1}, V)$. The assumption in (5.4) will be referred to as the *no early exclusion hypothesis* (NEEH), because it states that no value of V will be revealed to be impossible prior to T.

Under NEEH, Bossaerts (1996) shows that the following obtains:

$$E\left[\frac{\lambda_{t-1}(V^*)}{\lambda_t(V^*)}|x_{t-1}, V^*\right] = 1. \qquad [5.5]$$

That is, conditional on V^*, the expectation of the ratio of the time $(t-1)$ posterior and the time t posterior ($t = 1, \ldots, T - 1$), both evaluated at V^*, equals one.

As in the case of Doob's martingale result, the proof of (5.5) is extremely simple:

$$\begin{aligned}
E\left[\frac{\lambda_{t-1}(V^*)}{\lambda_t(V^*)}|x_t, V^*\right] &= \int \frac{\lambda_{t-1}(V^*)}{\lambda_t(V^*)} l_t(x|x_{t-1}, V^*)dx \\
&= \int \frac{\lambda_{t-1}(V^*) \int l_t(x|x_{t-1}, v)\lambda_{t-1}(v)dv}{l_t(x|x_{t-1}, V^*)\lambda_{t-1}(V^*)} l_t(x|x_{t-1}, V^*)dx \\
&= \int \int l_t(x|x_{t-1}, v)dx\, \lambda_{t-1}(v)dv \\
&= 1.
\end{aligned}$$

Despite (or perhaps because of) its simplicity, (5.5) generates easily verifiable empirical restrictions on the pricing of securities under ELM. Let us turn to those now.

5.3 Digital Option Prices under ELM

Let us use the stochastic structure from the previous section, whereby we let the market be the Bayesian learner.

That is, the market is asked to predict the outcome of a random variable V, to be revealed at T. At t, it receives signals in the form of what we have been referring to as the state vector x_t. It knows the likelihood function of the state given the final outcome. Its prior, however, is arbitrary. That is, ELM holds.

Assume for the moment that the market is risk neutral, and applies a zero discount rate. Later, we reintroduce risk aversion. The assumptions of risk neutrality and zero discounting allow us to focus on the effects of learning on security price behavior. Under risk neutrality and zero discounting, the price of a security is simply the expected payout, where expectations are obviously taken with respect to the subjective beliefs of the market.

The payoff on the security depends on V. In particular, consider a *digital option* that pays one dollar if $V = V^*$, and zero otherwise. The AD (state) securities that we have been using in earlier chapters are examples of digital options. Hence, the time t price of the digital option, P_t, equals the time-t posterior evaluated at V^*:

$$P_t = E^m[1_{\{V=V^*\}}|x_t, x_{t-1}, \ldots] = \lambda_t(V^*),$$

where $1_{\{\cdot\}}$ denotes the indicator function, which equals one if the condition in the brackets is satisfied, and zero otherwise.

From (5.5), we immediately obtain the following restriction on the dynamics of the digital option price:

$$E\left[\frac{P_{t-1}}{P_t}|x_{t-1}, V^*\right] = 1, \qquad [5.6]$$

provided, of course, NEEH holds. That is, the *inverse return* on winning digital options must not be predictable from past information. A *winning* digital option is one that will factually pay one dollar at the terminal date. The restriction in (5.5) is easy to verify. One simply collects price histories for winning digital options, computes sample average inverse returns, or projects inverse returns onto lagged information.

Notice that (5.5) confirms a conjecture that we made in the Introduction to this chapter, namely, that our tests must somehow work on biased samples. Indeed, to test (5.5), we only need the records of winning digital options. We need not bother about the losers; we also do not need to know the proportion of winners to losers.

Nor do we have to estimate the market's prior. In fact, tests of (5.5) inherit the elegance of tests of EMH, where we also had only to compute sample averages of readily available data or projections onto lagged information. Of course, when we assumed risk aversion, we also had to estimate conditional covariances. But, for the moment, we take the market to be risk neutral.

Nonzero discounting can easily be accommodated by scaling the option prices with the inverse of the discount factor (i.e., deflating). It turns out that risk aversion can also be incorporated in the analysis by means of scaling. We are not ready to do so yet: we must first investigate the price dynamics of general limited-liability securities under ELM. We can then reintroduce risk aversion and at the same time allow for nonzero discounting.

Are there restrictions on the price dynamics of losing digital options (i.e., those that end up paying zero dollars)? Although the answer is affirmative, more conditions are needed. For example, realizations of the state vector x_t must be independent over time (which is quite restrictive indeed). The interested reader is referred to Bossaerts (1996) and Bossaerts (2000).

5.4 Limited Liability Security Prices under ELM

Now we continue with the same stochastic framework, but introduce an asset that pays V if $V > 0$ and zero otherwise. This is the canonical form of a limited-liability security. Examples of such securities include equity and put and call options. The digital options of the previous section are a special case (think of V as a binary random variable: $V \in \{0, 1\}$).

With limited-liability securities, there are two basic states to be distinguished: (1) $V > 0$, (2) $V \leq 0$. Depending on the security, the state under (1) is referred to as *in the money* (options), or *no default/no bankruptcy* (equity). State (2) is referred to as *out of the money* (options), or *default/bankruptcy* (equity). We will simply call (2) the *default state*, and (1) the *no default state*, independent of the actual limited-liability asset at hand.

Under risk neutrality and zero discounting, the price of a limited-liability security equals the subjective conditional expectation of its payoff:

$$P_t = E^m[V1_{\{V>0\}}|x_t, x_{t-1}, \ldots]. \qquad [5.7]$$

We are aiming for a result similar to (5.6). We cannot derive the desired contraints without making one additional assumption about the beliefs of the market.

The additional assumption we need is one of *unbiased conditional beliefs (UCB): the market knows the mean of V conditional on no default*, or:

$$E^m[V|x_t, x_{t-1}, \ldots, V > 0] = E[V|x_t, x_{t-1}, \ldots, V > 0]. \quad [5.8]$$

Note that we are not conditioning on the actual value of V, but only on the event $V > 0$.

UCB effectively means the following. The market holds an unspecified prior about the probability of default (i.e., the event $V > 0$). This prior may be wrong. That is, the actual incidence of default may differ from the market's ex ante expectations. The market updates its prior as information about the eventual outcome is revealed. The updating uses Bayes' law, and is based on (1) the correct likelihood of signals given the final outcome, and (2) the correct expectation of the payoff, given no default. Notice that the market's ex ante expectations of other aspects than the mean of the payoff (conditional on no default) need not be right. For instance, the market may err about the range of possible payoffs, or its variance (conditional on no default).

Under UCB, the pricing formula (5.7) can be rewritten. To simplify notation, let:

$$\lambda_t(\{V > 0\}) = \int_0^\infty \lambda_t(v)\,dv.$$

Then:

$$
\begin{aligned}
P_t &= E^m[V1_{\{V>0\}}|x_t, x_{t-1}, \ldots] \\
&= E^m[V|x_t, x_{t-1}, \ldots, V > 0]\lambda_t(\{V > 0\}) \\
&= E[V|x_t, x_{t-1}, \ldots, V > 0]\lambda_t(\{V > 0\}). \quad [5.9]
\end{aligned}
$$

This allows us to derive the following surprising result, first stated in Bossaerts (2000). Under NEEH and UCB:

$$\boxed{E\left[\frac{P_t - P_{t-1}}{P_t}V|x_{t-1}, V > 0\right] = 0.} \quad [5.10]$$

That is, when computed with the future price as basis, the weighted rate of return of winning limited-liability securities is not predictable from past information. The weighting is given by the eventual payoff. A *winning* limited-liability security is one that did not default.

(We can apply this to a digital option, by taking V to be binary: $V \in (0, V^* = 1)$. (5.10) becomes:

$$E\left[\frac{P_t - P_{t-1}}{P_t}|x_{t-1}, V = V^* = 1\right] = 0.$$

Of course, this is but a restatement of (5.6)!)

The proof of (5.10) is an application of (5.5) to the event $V > 0$ (last equality below), after repeated appeal to the law of iterated expectations (all previous equalities):

$$E\left[\frac{P_t - P_{t-1}}{P_t}V|x_{t-1}, V > 0\right]$$

$$= E[V|x_{t-1}, V > 0] - E\left[\frac{P_{t-1}}{P_t}E[V|x_t, x_{t-1}, \ldots, V > 0]\right.$$

$$\left.|x_{t-1}, x_{t-2}, \ldots, V > 0\right]$$

$$= E[V|x_{t-1}, V > 0] - E\left[\frac{\lambda_{t-1}(\{V > 0\})}{\lambda_t(\{V > 0\})}\frac{E[V|x_{t-1}, \ldots, V > 0]}{E[V|x_t, x_{t-1}, \ldots, V > 0]}\right.$$

$$\left. E[V|x_t, x_{t-1}, \ldots, V > 0]|x_{t-1}, x_{t-2}, \ldots, V > 0\right]$$

$$= E[V|x_{t-1}, V > 0] - E\left[\frac{\lambda_{t-1}(\{V > 0\})}{\lambda_t(\{V > 0\})}\right.$$

$$\left. E[V|x_{t-1}, \ldots, V > 0]|x_{t-1}, x_{t-2}, \ldots, V > 0\right]$$

$$= E[V|x_{t-1}, x_{t-2}, \ldots, V > 0]$$

$$\left(1 - E\left[\frac{\lambda_{t-1}(\{V > 0\})}{\lambda_t(\{V > 0\})}|x_{t-1}, x_{t-2}, \ldots, V > 0\right]\right)$$

$$= 0.$$

The simplicity of (5.10) is remarkable. Because it involves only directly observable variables (i.e., prices and payoffs) and because it only restricts the actual (i.e., true) moments of these variables, it is readily verified on historical data. One merely needs a cross-section of histories of winners (i.e., limited-liability securities that did not default in the time series at hand).

Moreover, (5.10) reveals that ELM can be tested on substantially biased samples. Only the price dynamics of winning limited-liability securities is restricted, so that we can discard the losers. This often happens naturally anyway: there is a tendency for survivorship bias, because historical datasets only cover winners. But one can say something about the losers as well. Because the restrictions obtain only under tighter assumptions on the likelihood function, we will not explore these here. The reader is referred to Bossaerts (1996) for details.

At this point, we should ask how to incorporate risk aversion and/or nonzero discounting. That is, how can we introduce a nontrivial asset-pricing model? We want to do so in a way such that the ensuing tests are robust to deleting relevant information in price setting. This did obtain for certain tests of asset-pricing theory under EMH. In Chapter 2, we emphasize that such a property is important for empirical research.

The easiest way to accommodate asset-pricing theory is to scale the prices with a cleverly chosen factor. To see this, start from our general asset-pricing formula, written in terms of an aggregate risk measure A_t (unlike in Chapter 1, we make timing explicit by means of the subscript t). This formula predicts that the price of the nth security will be set such that its return satisfies the following stochastic Euler equation:

$$E^m[A_t R_{n,t} | x_{t-1}] = 1. \tag{5.11}$$

This is (1.32) of Chapter 1 (see also (2.23)), but we make explicit the subjectivity of the market's expectations, through the superscript m.

Remember that a choice of asset-pricing model fixes the risk measure A_t. For instance, in Lucas' model:

$$A_t = \delta \frac{\frac{\partial \tilde{u}(c_{A,t})}{\partial c}}{\frac{\partial \tilde{u}(c_{A,t-1})}{\partial c}},$$

where $c_{A,t}$ and $c_{A,t-1}$ denote aggregate consumption at t and $t-1$, respectively (see (1.28)). In Rubinstein's model:

$$A_t = \frac{1}{R_{M,t}},$$

where $R_{M,t}$ denotes the return on the market portfolio (see (1.29)).

Now write (5.11) in terms of prices, deleting the subscript n (which merely identifies the security):

$$E^m[A_t P_t | x_{t-1}] = P_{t-1}. \tag{5.12}$$

Adding past information does no harm:

$$E^m[A_t P_t | x_{t-1}, x_{t-2}, \ldots] = P_{t-1}. \tag{5.13}$$

Apply this to the pricing at times T and $T - 1$:

$$E^m[A_T P_T | x_{T-1}, x_{T-2}, \ldots] = P_{T-1}.$$

(Of course, with limited-liability securities,

$$P_T = V1_{\{V>0\}}.)$$

Because $A_{T-1}, A_{T-2}, \ldots, A_0$ are all in the market's information set at time $T - 1$, we could as well have written:

$$E^m[A_T A_{T-1} A_{T-2} \ldots A_0 P_T | x_{T-1}, x_{T-2}, \ldots] = A_{T-1} A_{T-2} \ldots A_0 P_{T-1}.$$

An analogous operation can be done at any prior point in time:

$$E^m[A_t A_{t-1} \ldots A_0 P_t | x_{t-1}, x_{t-2}, \ldots] = A_{t-1} \ldots A_0 P_{t-1}.$$

Consequently, if we *scale* the price at t by the factor $A_t A_{t-1} \ldots A_0$, and refer to the scaled price as $\tilde{P}_t$:

$$\tilde{P}_t = A_t A_{t-1} \ldots A_0 P_t, \qquad [5.14]$$

then the fundamental asset-pricing restriction in (5.12) becomes:

$$E^m[\tilde{P}_t | x_t, x_{t-1}, \ldots] = \tilde{P}_{t-1}.$$

Iterating, one obtains:

$$\tilde{P}_t = E^m[\tilde{P}_T | x_t, x_{t-1}, \ldots], \qquad [5.15]$$

with:

$$\tilde{P}_T = A_T A_{T-1} \ldots A_0 P_T = A_T A_{T-1} \ldots A_0 V1_{\{V>0\}}.$$

If we now define:

$$\tilde{V} = A_T A_{T-1} \ldots A_0 V, \qquad [5.16]$$

then our analysis remains intact, provided we substitute the scaled (i.e., deflated) prices $\tilde{P}_t$ for the actual prices P_t, and the scaled payoff $\tilde{V}$ for the actual payoff. In particular, (5.10) continues to hold, after suitable replacement:

$$\boxed{E\left[\frac{\tilde{P}_t - \tilde{P}_{t-1}}{\tilde{P}_t} \tilde{V} | x_{t-1}, x_{t-2}, \ldots, \tilde{V} > 0\right] = 0.} \qquad [5.17]$$

That is, weighted returns computed with scaled prices (and with the future scaled price as basis) of winning limited-liability securities are not predictable from past information. The weighting is based on the scaled payoff at the end of the history, that is, at T.

Besides the tildes on top of all variables, there is another difference between (5.10) and (5.17), which is of no real consequence: in (5.17), we condition on $x_{t-2}, \dots$ as well. We need this, because the scaling factors are functions of information further in the past as well. For instance, the scaling factor for the time t price, $A_t A_{t-1} \dots A_0$, is a function of x_{t-1}, x_{t-2}, and so on, and not merely a function of x_t. Mathematically, we introduced the additional conditioning in the analysis leading to (5.13).

Notice that the restriction in (5.17) remains even if we condition on a subset of the market's information, that is, on a subvector of x_{t-1} (or x_{t-2}, x_{t-3}, etc.), by the law of iterated expectations. In Chapter 2, we emphasized that this is a desirable property of any test of asset-pricing theory. It obtained only for certain tests of asset-pricing theory under EMH. It does obtain for tests of asset-pricing theory under ELM that are based on (5.17).

At this point, we should illustrate (5.17) with a numerical example.

5.5 Revisiting an Earlier Example

We build on the example from Chapter 2, page 47 where we priced equity in a firm subject to bankruptcy risk, using Rubinstein's model.

Recall that each period was split in two subperiods, "January" (J) and "the rest of the year" (O). In January, firms (indexed by n) do not declare bankruptcy, but a signal s_n indicates the likelihood of eventual bankruptcy, as well as the end-of-year payoff if the firm does not default. (To avoid confusion, we drop the index t from Chapter 2, where it counted years.) At the end of the year, firms may declare bankruptcy, at which point the equityholders receive zero dollars. The end-of-year payoff on the market portfolio is the product of a signal announced after January, s_M, and another, binomial random variable, θ_M. That of equity in firm n is the product of s_n, θ_n, $(s_M)^2$ and $(\theta_M)^2$. Thus, s_M also provides information about the end-of-year payoff on equity in firm n, if the firm does not default.

Let us map this into the notation of the present chapter. Clearly, the end-of-year payoff on firm n corresponds to V:

$$V = s_n \theta_n (s_M)^2 (\theta_M)^2.$$

There are two periods, J and O, and therefore, three points in time. Using t to denote time, $t = 0$ corresponds to the beginning of January, $t = 1$ corresponds to the beginning of O and $t = 2 = T$ corresponds to the end of the year. P_t corresponds to firm n's price at t. Of course, $P_T = V$. P_0 is firm n's price at the beginning of J, and P_1 is its price at the beginning of O.

Since we used Rubinstein's model in the pricing, A_t is the inverse return on the market portfolio (see (1.29)). Let $R_{M,t}$ denote the return on the market portfolio over the interval $(t - 1, t)$. Then:

$$A_t = \frac{1}{R_{M,t}},$$

where $t = 1, 2$. We set $A_0 = 1$. This can be used to scale prices and payoffs, as in (5.14) and (5.16):

$$\tilde{P}_0 = P_0,$$
$$\tilde{P}_1 = \frac{1}{R_{M,1}} P_1,$$
$$\tilde{V} = \frac{1}{R_{M,2} R_{M,1}} V.$$

We should now verify whether (5.17) obtains, that is, whether weighted returns computed from scaled prices (and payoffs) and with the future price as basis is zero on average. This we do for winners only, of course.

But notice that (5.17) requires (1) NEEH and (2) UCB. To ensure (1), we will use the conditional probabilities from Chapter 2 when computing the expectation in (5.17). That is, we assume that the actual probabilities of final payout given no default are identical to those used by the market to price the security. As far as (1) is concerned, however, note that NEEH fails during O, because the firm announces its bankruptcy status at the end of the year. But NEEH does obtain during J, because we did not allow the firm to announce default at the end of J; and thus only a noisy signal can be given (namely, s_n). Consequently, we expect (5.17) to hold only over J, but not over O.

Tedious calculations confirm that:

$$E\left[\frac{\tilde{P}_1 - \tilde{P}_0}{\tilde{P}_1}\tilde{V}|\tilde{V} > 0\right] = 0.$$

That is, (5.17) obtains over J. There is no state vector in this expression, because there is nothing to be conditioned on at the beginning of J.

In the Exercises, the reader is asked to prove that, under NEEH and UCB:

$$E\left[\frac{\tilde{P}_t - \tilde{P}_{t-1}}{\tilde{P}_t}|x_{t-1}, \tilde{V} > 0\right] \leq 0. \qquad [5.18]$$

That is, the *unweighted* return of winning limited-liability securities, computed from scaled prices and using the future price as basis, is nonpositive on average.

In the numerical example, explicit calculation shows that:

$$E\left[\frac{\tilde{P}_1 - \tilde{P}_0}{\tilde{P}_1}|\tilde{V} > 0\right] = -0.18 < 0,$$

thus confirming the theory.

In contrast, our results should not obtain over O, because NEEH is violated. To confirm this, imagine that the state of the world at the end of J is $(s_n, s_M) = (1, 0.9)$. Conditional on no default $(\theta_n = 1)$, there are only two possible outcomes at the end of the year $(t = 2)$, distinguished by whether θ_M equals 0.9 or 1.2. From the numerical data in Chapter 2, the latter possibilities occur with probability 0.6 and 0.4, respectively. The scaled price $\tilde{P}_1$ equals:

$$\tilde{P}_1 = \frac{1}{R_{M,1}}P_1 = \frac{1}{0.9}0.72 = 0.80.$$

The scaled final price (or payoff) $\tilde{V}$ equals:

$$\tilde{V} = \frac{1}{R_{M,1}}\frac{1}{R_{M,2}}V$$

$$= \begin{cases} \frac{1}{0.9}\frac{0.9}{(0.9)(0.9)}0.9^4 & \text{if } \theta_M = 0.9 \\ \frac{1}{0.9}\frac{0.9}{(0.9)(1.2)}0.9^2 1.2^2 & \text{if } \theta_M = 1.2 \end{cases}$$

$$= \begin{cases} 0.81 & \text{if } \theta_M = 0.9 \\ 1.08 & \text{if } \theta_M = 1.2. \end{cases}$$

Remembering that $\tilde{P}_2 = \tilde{V}$ this implies:

$$E\left[\frac{\tilde{P}_2 - \tilde{P}_1}{\tilde{P}_2} \tilde{V} | (s_n, s_M) = (1, 0.9), \tilde{V} > 0\right]$$
$$= E[\tilde{P}_2 - \tilde{P}_1 | (s_n, s_M) = (1, 0.9), \tilde{V} > 0]$$
$$= (0.6)(0.81 - 0.80) + (0.4)(1.08 - 0.80)$$
$$= 0.12 \neq 0.$$

Hence, (5.17) is violated. As an exercise, the reader can verify that (5.17) is violated in all states at $t = 1$, and hence, unconditionally as well.

Our numerical example should clarify the distinction between ELM and EMH. In computing the expectations that verified (5.17) and (5.18), we used all probabilities except the unconditional probability of default (i.e., the probability that $\theta_n = 0$). Indeed, we only calculated expectations conditional on no default, thereby avoiding any reference to the unconditional probability of no default. The latter was used only to compute prices.

Consequently, the true probability of default may differ from the numbers we used to compute prices. That is, the market's ex ante expectations may be wrong. But this will not affect the results. In fact, the empiricist does not even have to estimate the actual frequency of default. The empiricist need only study the price histories of limited-liability securities that did not default.

But our restrictions did not obtain over O. This is attributed to violations of NEEH. In some empirical contexts, assuming NEEH may be annoying. For instance, the historical record of equity prices may be affected by violations of NEEH, because firms can declare bankruptcy at any moment in time. That is, the requirement in our example that firms not announce default in J is generally irreal.

One would like to assess the impact of violations of NEEH on our results. It is hard to do this theoretically, because violations of NEEH generally result in ill-defined conditional expectations (see the discussion surrounding (5.3)). Our numerical example might lead one to believe that the impact can be dramatic. Simulations demonstrate the contrary, however, provided that the ex ante probability of default announcement over any period is low (see Bossaerts [1996]). One way to reduce the probability of default announcement over one period is to decrease the length of a period (i.e., increase the frequency of observations).

In Chapter 6, we study the post-issue performance of U.S. IPOs on the basis of the results we have derived so far. In the case of IPOs, bankruptcy announcements can be made at any point in time. Hence, NEEH does not hold. We work with monthly data, however. One could conjecture that the probability of bankruptcy announcement over one month is sufficiently low for violations of NEEH not to have a measurable impact.[36] We find that the restrictions we derived here, and hence, ELM, receive overwhelming support in the IPO data, except for a category of IPOs that we will identify later. Hence, the conjecture seems to enjoy empirical sympathy.

5.6   Conclusion

This chapter has demonstrated that asset-pricing theory can be tested with substantially weaker assumptions about market beliefs and stationarity than EMH. Despite relaxed assumptions, the tests retain simplicity, robustness, and sparse use of information. Historical datasets, however, have to be viewed as cross-sections of shorter histories, because the tests focus on transition, and not on averages over long periods of time. They essentially ask whether the observed price changes are compatible with an asset-pricing model and the view that the market updates its beliefs on the basis of the correct likelihood. Because the market may have otherwise largely unspecified beliefs, we referred to the collection of assumptions on beliefs and learning as the theory of efficiently learning markets (ELM).

This chapter presented only one application of ELM. Another one can be found in Bossaerts (1998), where the goal is to determine the correctness of a particular specification of the prior together with an asset-pricing model. Discussion of this second application is rather technical, however. Therefore, we should return to the data, and demonstrate that we can learn something useful with the theoretical results obtained so far.

36. Table 3.2 documents that about 17 percent of IPOs disappear over the first three years because of default (the category "Unknown" is included with "Liquidations" to get this number). If the occurrence of default follows a Poisson process, then the probability that default is announced in any month is $0.17/36 = 0.66$ percent, quite low indeed.

Exercises

1. Prove Doob's martingale result, (5.2).
2. Verify that (5.17) holds over J in the numerical example on page 148.
3. Derive a result analogous to (5.17) when default occurs when $V \leq D$ $(D > 0)$, at which point D is paid.
4. Prove (5.18).

CHAPTER 6

Revisiting the Historical Record

6.1 Introduction

Armed with new methodology, we are in a position to reconsider the historical field data. We are now able to test asset-pricing theory, not with EMH as the auxiliary assumption, but with ELM. That is, the market still must update its beliefs correctly (meaning that it uses Bayes' law and the right likelihood function), but need not hold correct expectations at the beginning of each history in the dataset.

Unlike tests of asset-pricing models based on EMH, work on ELM is only in its initial stages. But the first results, some of which we will discuss here, appear promising. The conclusions one can draw are intriguing. They shed new light on price setting in financial markets.

In this chapter, we conclude that there were no anomalies in the overall post-issue performance of U.S. IPOs in the period 1975–95, thus overturning the well-known conclusion from Ritter (1991) first mentioned in Chapter 3. The underperformance that Ritter (1991) reports seems to be entirely caused by biases, operating at the time of the IPO, of the market's expectation about default. These biases may be period-specific. That is, they may not repeat. Note that biases are plausible, because IPOs often occur in new industries, where the market may not yet have grasped the nature of either the technology or the economics.

The asset-pricing model we use to draw our conclusion is extremely simple. It is Rubinstein's log-CAPM, discussed in Chapter 1 (see (1.29)). This means that U.S. IPOs in 1975–95 were priced as if there was a representative agent with logarithmic utility, who found it optimal to hold the market portfolio. To put this differently: IPO expected returns were proportional to the covariance with a hyperbolic function of the return on the market.

We discover, however, convincing rejections in one surprising sub-category: low-priced issues (i.e., IPOs issued at a price of six dollars or less). We do not delve into interpreting the rejections: a great deal of work still needs to be done to come up with plausible explanations. Among other things, we must first better understand the nature of a market where neither EMH nor ELM holds. Ideas are suggested in Bossaerts and Hillion (2001), on which this chapter is based.

In evaluating the empirical results we are about to discuss, the reader should take into account the pre-publication history of the journal article on which this chapter is based, namely, Bossaerts and Hillion (2001). Working paper versions of the article were based on IPOs in Ritter's original time frame, 1975–84. The tests supported ELM. The editor and a referee then requested an extension of the dataset, essentially asking for a replication of the results on a sample that turned out to be three times larger. The only effect of tripling the sample size was a tightening of the confidence intervals.

Let us discuss the evidence.

6.2   U.S. IPO Aftermarket Performance

We take the dataset studied in Ritter (1991), covering U.S. IPOs in the period 1975–84. We test Rubinstein's model in conjunction with ELM on an extended version of this dataset, discussed in Bossaerts and Hillion (2001). A total of 4,848 histories covering the period 1975–1995 are included. Five years of monthly post-issue returns are studied.[37] Of course,

---

37. Bossaerts and Hillion (2001) investigate histories up to ten years' duration. The IPOs floated in 1995 are followed for only three years, and those floated in 1994 for only four years.

Table 6.1

The Fate of U.S. IPOs One to Five Years after Issue, 1975–95

Reference Point	Categories[1]				
	Active	Mergers	Exchanges	Liquidations	Unknown
One year	4,780	22	3	29	14
	(98.6)[2]	(0.5)	(0.1)	(0.6)	(0.3)
Two years	4,388	179	13	205	63
	(90.5)	(3.7)	(0.3)	(4.2)	(1.3)
Three years	3,932	360	22	419	115
	(81.1)	(7.4)	(0.5)	(8.6)	(2.4)
Four years[3]	3,260	529	33	609	139
	(71.3)	(11.6)	(0.7)	(13.3)	(3.0)
Five years[4]	2,649	675	45	794	153
	(61.4)	(15.6)	(1.0)	(18.4)	(3.5)

[1]Categories: (i) *Active* issues: CRSP delisting code (DC) 100; (ii) *Mergers*: DCs 200–203; (iii) *Exchanges*: DCs 300–390; (iv) *Liquidations* (and forced delistings): DCs 550–588, 400 and 700; (v) *Unknown* (and inactive): DCs 500–520.

[2]Numbers in brackets: percentage of total.

[3]From year 4 on, the sample excludes 278 IPOs floated in 1995.

[4]From year 5 on, the sample excludes 254 IPOs floated in 1994 as well.

many of these histories are incomplete, because of delisting caused by mergers, acquisitions or exchanges, liquidations, or for other reasons.

Because the probability of default is at the heart of the methodology that tests ELM, Table 6.1 extends the earlier Table 3.2, which documented the attrition in the dataset for three years after issue. After five years, only 61 percent of the IPOs is still available as a separate issue. Almost 22 percent have been liquidated or disappeared because of unknown cause. This underscores the importance of default, and hence, the necessity of a methodology that allows the market to hold mistaken expectations about the frequency and distribution over time of default. Mistakes will have a large impact on price dynamics. Our methodology is well suited to accommodate such forecasting mistakes.

Our methodology is not entirely appropriate for a study of IPO aftermarket performance, because it assumes NEEH, which means that all outcomes (including default) should never be excluded early on. To see this, fix a reference date (T in Chapter 5), say, at forty-eight months. Study the weighted average returns of the winners (i.e., those that did not default by the forty-eighth month; see (5.17)) over the first forty-two months. Then we actually require that default never be announced before the forty-third month. Such is not the case, of course. But we also mentioned in the previous chapter that simulations demonstrate that the restrictions predicted by the theory of ELM—in particular, (5.17)—become approximately correct if the probability of early revelation of the final state is small. In the case of IPOs, the probability of early announcement of default in any month up to four years is $(0.13 + 0.03)/48 = 0.33$ percent, quite low indeed (a Poisson process is assumed, and the Unknown category is included with the Liquidations).

Also, in accordance with the theoretical developments of Chapter 5, we assume that an issue becomes worthless upon default. It is known that shareholders do often receive something, but the exact numbers are not in our records. This being said, we could have accommodated nonzero liquidation values. See the Exercises at the end of Chapter 5.

Because we assume that Rubinstein's model holds, we should re-evaluate the post-issue performance. This time, we should not compare the cumulative average return against that of carefully matched firms, as in Fig. 3.9, but against that of the market portfolio. As a proxy of the market portfolio, we again use the value-weighted Center for Research in Securities Prices (CRSP) index. Figure 6.1 displays the result. The underperformance is still phenomenal. After five years, the cumulative average excess return is about −40 percent. Can we explain this underperformance with (1) Rubinstein's model, and (2) mistaken expectations about default at the IPO date? The answer is based on the weighted average modified risk-adjusted returns of the winners.

Let us demonstrate that the answer is affirmative. Under ELM, the weighted average modified risk-adjusted return of winners should be zero on average. The weighting is based on the risk-adjusted payoff at some future date. The return is computed with the future price (end-of-month) as basis. To adjust for risk, we deflate prices and payoffs appropriately, using Rubinstein's model; see (5.11) and the subsequent discussion, especially (5.14) and (5.16). For comparison purposes, we also present returns computed in the standard way, with the risk-adjusted price at the beginning of the month as basis. To distinguish the two, we refer to the former as the *modified* return.

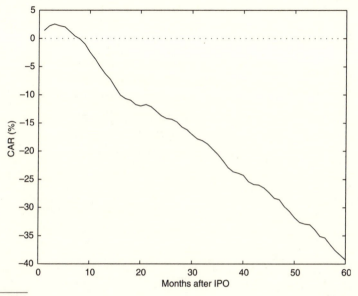

Figure 6.1

Cumulative average monthly returns (CAR) on 4,848 U.S. IPOs in the period
1975–95, in excess of the cumulative average monthly return on the
value-weighted CRSP index, excluding the first day of trading.

Winners are defined to be IPOs that at the reference date (i.e., the
horizon) were either active, merged or exchanged. See Table 6.1. If
merged or exchanged, we take the reference value to be the wealth that
would have been generated if the issue was sold at the end of the last
month before the acquisition date and invested in a riskfree security
(e.g., rolled-over three-month T-bills). As horizon (T in the previous
chapter), we take one, two, three, four and five years after the issue date.
We compute monthly returns (standard as well as modified) for all the
months since the issue date (but not including the first day after an issue),
up to six months before the reference date. All this implements a test
based on the restriction in (5.17).

Figure 6.2 displays the results. It plots sample average weighted modified returns for all the winners in the sample of 4,848 IPOs (vertical
bars) as well as 95 percent confidence intervals (horizontal bars) for the
different horizons. For comparison, the corresponding standard average

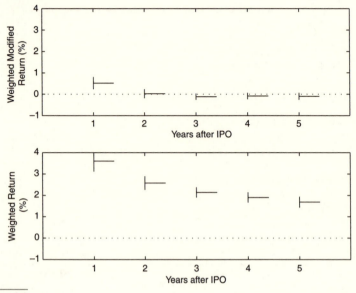

Figure 6.2

One-month weighted average risk-adjusted returns (horizontal bars) and 98 percent confidence intervals (vertical bars) on 4,848 U.S. IPOs in the period 1975–95, for different horizons, winners only. Top panel, weighted modified return. Bottom panel, usual return. Modified return is computed with end-of-month risk-adjusted price as basis. Risk adjustment is based on Rubinstein's model.

returns and 95 percent confidence intervals are also plotted. The reader can verify that failure to reject ELM is not due to weighting with a potentially noisy variable, namely, the risk-adjusted IPO value at the horizon date. Because we look at winners only, the average standard returns should be affected by selection bias. In particular, they should be significantly positive if the average standard returns in the entire sample are zero (in fact, they were negative—see Fig. 6.1). And they are, for all horizons.

Except for a horizon of one year (when returns are computed on the basis of the first six months after the IPO), the weighted modified excess return is never significantly different from zero. This provides support for ELM and Rubinstein's model. The significantly positive standard weighted excess returns should suggest that the support must not be attributable to using noisy weights. Notice also that the confidence intervals are tight.

Since ELM cannot be rejected (Fig. 6.2), whereas EMH must be (Fig. 6.1), the IPO post-issue underperformance must be attributed to mistakes in the market's expectations about default at the issue date. The results demonstrate the relevance of ELM as a way to explain alleged anomalies in financial markets. That we can establish this with a simple asset-pricing model—Rubinstein's—underscores that learning dominates the dynamics of asset prices.

Although the picture obtained from the entire IPO sample favors the view of a market that learns according to the rules of ELM, and that prices IPOs according to Rubinstein's model, solid evidence against this view emerges when considering sub-categories. From the many sub-categories one can construct (see Bossaerts and Hillion [2001]), two generate systematic rejections. Of these two, the first one, based on the issue underpricing, is least convincing, though.

Figure 6.3 plots the one-month average weighted modified risk-adjusted returns for the decile of IPOs that experienced the largest price runup on the first day after the IPO date, as measured from the issue price. The top panel presents a well-known result: these IPOs (commonly referred to as *hot IPOs*) generate large, significantly negative risk-adjusted returns, if not in the first six months, then afterwards. That amounts to a solid rejection of EMH (in conjunction with Rubinstein's model). The picture is better when cast in terms of the weighted modified risk-adjusted return of the winners only, although it is not perfect. The evidence against ELM (and Rubinstein's model) is less convincing than that against EMH: at the five-year horizon, the weighted modified risk-adjusted return on winners is only one-third the risk-adjusted return on all issues.

In fact, the dismal post-issue performance of low-priced IPOs is far more significant, even when measured in terms of weighted modified risk-adjusted returns. This is true for all IPOs in the first three deciles, where the deciles are constructed on the basis of issue price level. The first three deciles correspond to IPOs that were priced at roughly six dollars and below.

Figure 6.4 plots the weighted modified risk-adjusted returns for these deciles for up to five years after the issue date. Admittedly, those with a

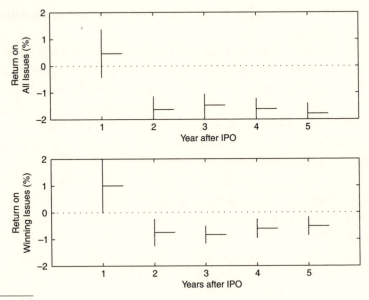

Figure 6.3

One-month average risk-adjusted returns (horizontal bars) and 95 percent confidence intervals (vertical bars) on "hot" IPOs in the period 1975–95, for different horizons. "Hot" IPOs belong to the top decile in terms of underpricing at the issue date. Top panel, standard risk-adjusted returns for all issues. Bottom panel, weighted modified risk-adjusted return for winners only; modified risk-adjusted return is computed with end-of-month risk-adjusted price as basis. Risk adjustment is based on Rubinstein's model.

horizon of one year (and hence, based on the first six months after issue) are insignificantly different from zero. But this may be the effect of lack of power. The weighted modified risk-adjusted returns are generally significantly negative for other horizons, and there is little sign that they improve as the horizon lengthens. Consequently, Figure 6.4 provides disturbing evidence against our conjecture that the market learns efficiently and prices IPOs according to Rubinstein's model.

We do not yet understand why low-priced issues generate aftermarket underperformance that cannot be attributed to biases in the market's expectation about default. There are many possible explanations. Our tests require UCB: the market is assumed to have held unbiased beliefs

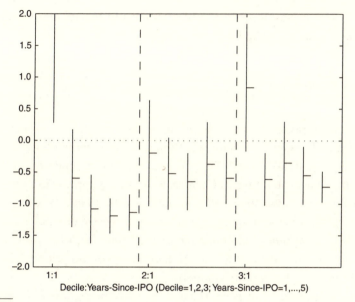

Figure 6.4

One-month average risk-adjusted returns (horizontal bars) and 95 percent confidence intervals (vertical bars) on low-priced U.S. IPOs in the period 1975–95, for different horizons. Low-priced IPOs belong to the first, second and third decile in terms of issue price level. Modified excess return is computed with end-of-month risk-adjusted price as basis. Risk adjustment is based on Rubinstein's model.

about the expected payoff, given a winner. UCB may have been violated over the period of the study. The market may just not have been capable of updating beliefs correctly (either it used a false likelihood or it ignored Bayes' law). Or Rubinstein's asset-pricing model is invalid. Future research should determine where the cause lies.

Are we certain that we collected all U.S. IPOs in the period 1975–95? Probably, we did not. In particular, we may be missing the worst cases: those that failed almost immediately. (The low failure rate in the first year after issue is suspicious—see Table 6.1.) But it does not matter. It would if we were testing asset-pricing theory based on EMH. ELM-based tests, however, are immune to biases caused by ignoring the losers. Only the records of winners are needed.

This means that evidence in support of ELM is far more robust than one could ever claim for tests of EMH.

6.3 Conclusion

We have presented an example that illustrates the econometric techniques developed in Chapter 5. Despite obvious limitations, the findings suggest that the methodology is promising. The methodology is based on a hypothesis about market beliefs, ELM, which appears to fit the historical record better than EMH. In other words, it appears to be more appropriate to model financial markets in the image of a Bayesian learner who may at times hold mistaken expectations, but who updates beliefs correctly. Surprisingly, with ELM, markets appear to price risk in a fairly simple way (Rubinstein's model).

A great deal of work remains to be done before ELM proves itself conclusively as an alternative to EMH in historical analysis of field financial-market data. The reader who is interested in additional empirical tests of asset pricing under ELM should consult Bondarenko (1997), Bondarenko and Bossaerts (2000), Bossaerts (1996), Bossaerts (1998), and Bossaerts (2000).

REFERENCES

Arrow, K. J. 1953. "Le rôle des valeurs boursières pour la répartition la meilleure des risques." "The Role of Securities in the Optimal Allocation of Risk Bearing." (Translation) *Review of Economic Studies* 31: 91–96.

Arrow, K., and F. Hahn. 1971. *General Competitive Analysis*. San Francisco: Holden-Day.

Banz, R. 1981. "The Relationship between Return and Market Value of Common Stocks." *Journal of Financial Economics* 9: 3–18.

Benink, H., and P. Bossaerts. 2001. "An Exploration of Neo-Austrian Theory Applied to Financial Markets." *Journal of Finance* 56: 1011–28.

Berk, J. 1995. "A Critique of Size-Related Anomalies." *Review of Financial Studies* 8: 275–86.

Berk, J., R. C. Green, and V. Naik. 1999. "Optimal Investment, Growth Options and Security Returns." *Journal of Finance*, 54: 1553–1607.

Bertsekas, D., and S. Shreve. 1976. *Stochastic Optimal Control: the Discrete Time Case*. New York: Academic Press.

Biais, B., and P. Bossaerts. 1998. "Asset Prices and Trading Volume in a Beauty Contest." *Review of Economic Studies* 65: 307–40.

Bondarenko, O. 1997. "Testing Rationality of Financial Markets: an Application to S&P 500 Index Options." Caltech Working Paper.

Bondarenko, O., and P. Bossaerts. 2000. "Expectations and Learning in Iowa." *Journal of Banking and Finance* 24: 1535–55.

Bossaerts, P. 1995. "The Econometrics of Learning in Financial Markets." *Econometric Theory* 11: 151–89.

———. 1996. "Martingale Restrictions on Securities Prices under Rational

Expectations and Consistent Beliefs." Caltech Working Paper.

————. 1998. "Learning and Securities Price Volatility." Caltech Working Paper.

————. 2000. "Filtering Returns for Unspecified Biases in Priors when Testing Asset Pricing Theory." Caltech Working Paper.

Bossaerts, P., L. Fine, and J. Ledyard. 2000. "Inducing Liquidity in Thin Financial Markets through Combined-Value Trading Mechanisms." Caltech Working Paper.

Bossaerts, P., and R. C. Green. 1989. "A General Equilibrium Model of Changing Risk Premia: Theory and Tests." *Review of Financial Studies* 2: 467–93.

Bossaerts, P., and P. Hillion. 1995. "Testing the Mean-Variance Efficiency of Well-Diversified Portfolios in Very Large Cross-Sections." *Annales d'Economie et de Statistique* 40: 93–124.

————. 2001. "IPO Post-Issue Markets: Questionable Predilections but Diligent Learners?" *Review of Economics and Statistics* 83: 333–47.

Bossaerts, P., and C. Plott. 1999. "Basic Principles of Asset Pricing Theory: Evidence from Large-Scale Experimental Financial Markets." Caltech Working Paper.

————. 2001. "The CAPM in Thin Experimental Financial Markets." *Journal of Economic Dynamics and Control.* Forthcoming.

Bossaerts, P., C. Plott, and W. Zame. 2000. "Prices and Allocations in Financial Markets: Theory and Evidence." Caltech Working Paper.

Breeden, D. T. 1979. "An Intertemporal Asset Pricing Model with Stochastic Consumption and Investment Opportunities." *Journal of Financial Economics* 7: 265–96.

Brennan, M., T. Chordia, and A. Subrahmanyam. 1998. "Survival." *Journal of Financial Economics* 49: 345–73.

Brown, S., W. Goetzmann, and S. Ross. 1995. "Survival." *Journal of Finance* 50: 853–74.

Campbell, J., and J. Cochrane. 1999. "By Force of Habit: a Consumption-Based Explanation of Aggregate Stock Market Behavior." *Journal of Political Economy* 107: 205–51.

Chamberlain, G. 1988. "Asset Pricing in Multiperiod Securities Markets." *Econometrica* 56: 1283–1300.

Chari, V. V., R. Jagannathan, and A. Offer. 1988. "Seasonalities in Security Returns: the Case of Earnings Announcements." *Journal of Financial Economics* 21: 101–22.

Chen, N., R. Roll, and S. Ross. 1986. "Economic Forces and the Stock Market." *Journal of Business* 59: 383–403.

Clower, R. 1967. "A Re-Consideration of the Microfoundations of Monetary Theory." *Western Economic Journal* 6: 1–9.

Cochrane, J. 1999. "New Facts in Finance." *NBER Working Paper Series,* 7169.

————. 2001. *Asset Pricing.* Princeton and Oxford: Princeton University Press.

Cohen, K. J., et al. 1983. "Friction in the Trading Process and the Estimation of Systematic Risk." *Journal of Financial Economics* 12: 263–78.

Constantinides, G. 1982. "Intertemporal Asset Pricing with Heterogeneous Consumers and without Demand Aggregation." *Journal of Business* 55: 253–67.

———. 1990. "Habit Formation: a Resolution of the Equity Premium Puzzle." *Journal of Political Economy* 98: 519–43.

Daniel, K., and S. Titman. 1997. "Evidence on the Characteristics of Cross-Sectional Variation in Common Stock Returns." *Journal of Finance* 52: 1–33.

Dann, L. 1981. "Common Stock Repurchases: an Analysis of Returns to Bond-holders and Stockholders." *Journal of Financial Economics* 9: 113–38.

Danthine, J., and J. Donaldson. 1999. "Non-Falsified Expectations and General Equilibrium Asset Pricing: the Power of the Peso." *Economic Journal* 109: 607–35.

Davis, J., E. Fama, and K. French. 2000. "Characteristics, Covariances, and Average Returns: 1929 to 1997." *Journal of Finance* 55: 389–406.

DeBondt, W., and R. Thaler. 1985. "Does the Stock Market Overreact?" *Journal of Finance* 40: 793–808.

Debreu, G. 1959. *Theory of Value.* New York: Wiley.

Doob, J. L. 1948. "Application of the Theory of Martingales." *Colloques Internationaux du CNRS* 36: 23–27.

Epstein, L., and S. Zin. 1991. "Substitution, Risk Aversion and the Temporal Behavior of Consumption and Asset Returns: an Empirical Analysis." *Journal of Political Economy* 99: 263–86.

Fama, E. 1970. "Efficient Capital Markets: a Review of Theory and Empirical Work." *Journal of Finance* 25: 383–417.

Fama, E., and K. French. 1992. "The Cross-section of Expected Stock Returns." *Journal of Finance* 47: 427–65.

———. 1996. "Multifactor Explanations of Asset Pricing Anomalies." *Journal of Finance* 51: 55–84.

Fama, E., and J. MacBeth. 1973. "Risk, Return and Equilibrium: Empirical Tests." *Journal of Political Economy* 71: 607–36.

Gallant, R. A., and G. Tauchen. 1996. "Which Moments to Match?" *Economic Theory* 12: 657–81.

Gibbons, M. 1982. "Multivariate Tests of Financial Models: a New Approach." *Journal of Financial Economics* 10: 3–27.

Gibbons, M., S. Ross, and J. Shanken. 1989. "A Test of the Efficiency of a Given Portfolio." *Econometrica* 57: 1121–52.

Glosten, L., and P. Milgrom. 1985. "Bid, Ask, and Transaction Prices in a Specialist Market with Heterogeneously Informed Traders." *Journal of Financial Economics* 14: 71–100.

Goetzmann, W., and P. Jorion. 1999. "Global Stock Markets in the Twentieth Century." *Journal of Finance* 54: 953–80.

Gouriéroux, C., A. Monfort, and E. Renault. 1993. "Indirect Inference." *Journal of Applied Econometrics* 8: S95–S118.

Grossman, S. J., and J. E. Stiglitz. 1980. "On the Impossibility of Informationally Efficient Markets." *American Economic Review* 70: 393–408.

Hansen, L., and R. Jagannathan. 1991. "Implications of Security Market Data for Models of Dynamic Economies." *Journal of Political Economy* 99: 225–62.

Hansen, L. P., and K. J. Singleton. 1982. "Generalized Instrumental Variables Estimation of Nonlinear Rational Expectations Models." *Econometrica* 50: 1269–86.

Harsanyi, J. C. 1967. "Games with Incomplete Information Played by 'Bayesian' Players (I)." *Management Science* 14: 159–82.

Hawawini, G., and D. Keim. 1998. "The Cross-Section of Common Stock Returns: a Review of the Evidence and Some Findings." INSEAD and Wharton School Working Paper.

Heaton, J., and D. Lucas. 2000. "Portfolio Choice and Asset Prices: the Importance of Entrepreneurial Risk." *Journal of Finance* 55: 1163–98.

Ibbotson, R. G. 1975. "Price Performance of Common Stock New Issues." *Journal of Financial Economics* 3: 235–72.

Jagannathan, R., and Z. Whang. 1996. "Yes, the CAPM Is Well and Alive." *Journal of Finance* 51: 3–53.

Jordan, J. S. 1985. "Learning Rational Expectations: the Finite State Case." *Journal of Economic Theory* 36: 257–76.

Judd, K., and S. Guu. 2000. "Bifurcation Methods for Asset Market Equilibrium Analysis." Hoover Institute Working Paper.

Kyle, A. P. 1985. "Continuous Auctions and Insider Trading." *Econometrica* 53: 1315–35.

Levy, H. 1997. "Risk and Return: an Experimental Analysis." *International Economic Review* 38: 119–49.

Lintner, J. 1965. "The Valuation of Risk Assets and the Selection of Risky Investments in Stock Portfolios and Capital Budgets." *Review of Economics and Statistics* 47: 13–37.

Lucas, R. 1978. "Asset Prices in an Exchange Economy." *Econometrica* 46: 1429–45.

———. 1982. "Interest Rates and Currency Prices in a Two-Country World." *Journal of Monetary Economics* 10: 335–59.

Lucas, R., and N. Stokey. 1989. *Recursive Methods in Economic Dynamics.* Cambridge, Mass.: Harvard University Press.

Marcet, A., and T. Sargent. 1989. "Convergence of Least Squares Learning Mechanisms in Self Referential Linear Stochastic Models." *Journal of Economic Theory* 48: 337–68.